PRAISE FOR M

"What a blessing Allen Parr is to the church and those seeking truth. Allen has been answering questions about Jesus and the Bible for years, and he's become a trusted resource for Christians and questioners alike. *Misled* will help you understand what's true about Christianity while it protects you from what's false. If you're a believer, get this book so you can discern truth from error. If you're a seeker, get it to answer your doubts. In either case, *Misled* will become a trusted resource for generations to come."

—J. Warner Wallace, *Dateline*-featured cold-case detective, senior fellow at the Colson Center for Christian Worldview, and author of *Cold-Case Christianity* and *Person of Interest*

"The problem with being deceived is that you don't know you're being deceived. Allen Parr brilliantly shines the light of truth on several deceptions that many Christians today believe. Get your highlighter out because Misled provides one insight after another as it leads you back to what true Christianity is all about. This is a great and timely book!"

—Frank Turek, founder of CrossExamined.org and author of *I Don't Have Enough Faith to Be an Atheist*

"Get ready to dive into a compelling and eye-opening read with this incredible book written by Allen Parr. As the world becomes more flooded with false preachers, *Misled* serves as a beacon of light for those seeking strong biblical teaching. You'll be amazed by Allen's journey and the wisdom God has given him through all his experiences. This is a must-read for anyone looking to deepen their faith and shield themselves from the cunning lies of Satan. So don't wait—pick up a copy of this book today and get ready to be enlightened and empowered!"

—Daniel Maritz, founder of DLM Christian Lifestyle and author of *Bold Pursuit*

"Throughout my reading of *Misled*, I found myself nodding and agreeing, sometimes out loud, with what Allen writes. I might have even clapped at one point. His approach is firm but fair, calling out the nonsense that can mislead Christians. He points us back to Scripture as the remedy and compass for truth. I have seen all these teachings sneak within Christian circles and churches. Allen succinctly points out the issues and how to equip yourself to avoid being taken captive by their empty promises and harmful doctrines. He has a way of expressing hard truths with love for the lost in mind. Buy two copies of this book. Keep one for yourself and give the other to someone susceptible to being misled."

—MELISSA DOUGHERTY, APOLOGIST, BLOGGER FOR
CROSSEXAMINED.ORG, AND VIDEO CONTENT CREATOR

"As a charismatic who believes in the gifts of the Spirit, I found this book extremely helpful and refreshing. Some critics may have falsely presumed that Allen is attempting to quench the Spirit or discourage the use of spiritual gifts, but after sitting with this book and hearing his heart, I can tell you that is far from true. Allen has laid out a brilliant overview of how operating within the guidelines of Scripture leads to truly walking by the Spirit. His concerns towards hyper charismania and progressive Christianity are warranted and timely. And his constant appeal to the gospel is why I call him brother and friend. I believe anyone who sits with *Misled* will be led into more robust truth and avoid a future shipwrecked faith."

—RUSLAN, CHRISTIAN YOUTUBER AND FOUNDER OF BLESS GOD STUDIOS

MISLED

7 LIES THAT DISTORT THE GOSPEL
(AND HOW YOU CAN DISCERN THE TRUTH)

ALLEN PARR

NELSON
BOOKS

An Imprint of Thomas Nelson

Misled

Published in Nashville, Tennessee, by Nelson Books, an imprint of Thomas Nelson. Nelson Books and Thomas Nelson are registered trademarks of HarperCollins Christian Publishing, Inc.

Thomas Nelson titles may be purchased in bulk for educational, business, fundraising, or sales promotional use. For information, please email SpecialMarkets@ThomasNelson.com.

Unless otherwise noted, Scripture quotations are taken from the Christian Standard Bible®, Copyright © 2017 by Holman Bible Publishers. Used by permission. Christian Standard Bible® and CSB® are federally registered trademarks of Holman Bible Publishers.

Scripture quotations marked ESV are taken from the ESV® Bible (The Holy Bible, English Standard Version®). Copyright © 2001 by Crossway, a publishing ministry of Good News Publishers. Used by permission. All rights reserved.

Scripture quotations marked NKJV are taken from the New King James Version®. Copyright © 1982 by Thomas Nelson. Used by permission. All rights reserved.

Scripture quotations marked NLT are taken from the Holy Bible, New Living Translation. © 1996, 2004, 2015 by Tyndale House Foundation. Used by permission of Tyndale House Publishers, Inc., Carol Stream, Illinois 60188. All rights reserved.

Any internet addresses, phone numbers, or company or product information printed in this book are offered as a resource and are not intended in any way to be or to imply an endorsement by Thomas Nelson, nor does Thomas Nelson vouch for the existence, content, or services of these sites, phone numbers, companies, or products beyond the life of this book.

ISBN 978-1-4002-3976-4 (eBook)
ISBN 978-1-4002-3975-7 (HC)
ISBN 978-1-4002-3983-2 (TP)

Library of Congress Control Number: 2023931441

Printed in the United States of America

24 25 26 27 28 LBC 5 4 3 2 1

*To my wife, Jennifer, the only woman in
the world I've ever truly loved.*

CONTENTS

FOREWORD

by Dr. Sean McDowell

A few years ago, I decided to try expanding my ministry through YouTube. Since my focus is on tackling tough questions to the Christian faith, I quickly discovered Allen Parr's channel. Two things immediately jumped out at me about Allen.

First, he is a cool, likable, and genuine guy. That's probably obvious to you too. Getting to know him personally has only confirmed my suspicions. Second, Allen is committed to tackling the most difficult issues of our day through a biblical lens. If you follow his ministry online, you know that he doesn't shy away from thorny cultural, theological, and moral issues, yet he consistently approaches them with biblical discernment.

It should be no surprise that his heart comes through in *Misled*. If you start following Allen's ministry online, you will find the same likable and genuine person in the pages of this book. In fact, he opens with an honest and heartfelt example about when he, as a college student, was *misled* into joining a toxic church. Even though it took him four years to leave, he learned some powerful (and painful) lessons that motivate much of his ministry and, in particular, the writing of this book.

One of the things I love about *Misled* is that Allen uses a narrative to frame each chapter. He introduces us to a fictional character named Jarren, who personally encounters false and dangerous doctrines, and *then* Allen takes us to Scripture for discernment. This not only makes the journey engaging, but it helps us as readers visualize how we might also be misled into believing false doctrines.

How might you read this book? Allow me to offer two suggestions.

First, *read with your Bible in hand.* As you have likely seen online, Allen always takes us back to Scripture. What happens if you disagree with one of his conclusions? Great! As long as the Bible is your authority and guide, I suspect Allen would be just fine with that. In fact, there's a few issues I would address differently than Allen does here. But I can tell you this: He made me think. He challenged me to examine my understanding of Scripture. Like the Bereans in Acts 17, *Misled* challenged me to search the Scriptures for truth. And it will do the same for you.

Second, *read with humility.* The point of this book is not to uncover false doctrines for the sake of "winning" arguments with our friends. Rather, it is to build up our own biblical discernment so we can lovingly engage those around us. Our first job is to not be misled, and then we can graciously help others.

Misled is a great book. I hope you will read it, study it, and discuss it with a friend.

Enjoy the journey.

INTRODUCTION

WHY I WROTE THIS BOOK

t was the spring of 1994, and I hadn't attended church my entire freshman year of college. I honestly had little interest in attending church since I didn't have to. I was too busy enjoying the freedom of being outside my parents' supervision. Although I grew up in church and knew right from wrong, I was struggling with lust and immorality. I never read my Bible. At the time, my sister was on fire for the Lord and kept trying to get me to experience the things she was experiencing, but I wasn't interested.

That is, until the deacon of a local church came to my college campus and offered to lead a Bible study for me and my friends on Friday nights. He seemed pretty cool, so my friends and I figured we'd entertain the idea and give him a chance. Little did I know that one seemingly insignificant decision would lead me into a toxic relationship with a local church that lasted more than four years.

Things started out great. The Friday night Bible studies ignited a fire within me to finally take my walk with God seriously. I started reading the Bible from time to time, and naturally I started attending the deacon's church. At first everything was so exciting and new. The worship and sermons brought me to tears each week as I wrestled with my fleshly desires and my new identity as a devoted follower of Christ. Later I joined the worship team and even had the opportunity to facilitate a small-group study of a discipleship curriculum called *Experiencing God.*

But soon I began noticing things that didn't line up with what I was reading in the Bible. For example, week after week I was being pressured to speak in tongues—and I began to feel out of place because I couldn't.

Church members often spoke in tongues with no interpretation, which left me confused. Even the pastor would break out in tongues in the middle of his sermon. The worship leader did the same during worship. I also encountered a phenomenon called "being slain in the Spirit": the pastors would lay hands on people and they would just fall down. I didn't know what was happening or why the pastors were doing this. At times they even tried forcing me to fall down and seemed annoyed or disappointed when I didn't. They interpreted this as resistance to the work of the Spirit and implied that I was stifling their anointing.

All of this made me feel extremely uncomfortable. But as is so often the case with those who experience abuse (whether spiritual or otherwise), I didn't know how to speak up or remove myself from the situation. To make matters worse, the pastor frequently spoke a prophetic word over my life, and because it came from a spiritual leader, I was expected to follow blindly. There was no room to question his spiritual authority.

The warning signs kept piling up. One day my friends and I went to the leaders of the church and confessed that we were struggling with sexual immorality. Instead of teaching us what the Bible said or providing practical guidance for breaking free from habitual sin, they invited us into a small back room, where they laid hands on us and prayed against the evil spirits of lust within us. The meeting turned into what some would call an exorcism. They were laying hands on us so aggressively that they left physical marks on my body as they sought to drive out the lustful demons.

At that point I knew this church had serious issues. All of the signs were there, but unfortunately I wasn't able to admit that I needed to get out. This church was the only spiritual home I knew. I was also afraid that if I left the church, God would be angry with me, and I would forfeit the blessings available only to those under the spiritual covering and authority of the church leaders.

I was being *misled*. Yet in spite of the false doctrine, the manipulation, and the abuse, I didn't have the strength to walk away. Then something else happened.

Rumors had been flying around for years that the pastor struggled with same-sex attraction. I initially shrugged it off. He was a tall, well-built, handsome man with a wife and two kids. I figured that the people spreading the rumors were either jealous or wanted to tear down his ministry. Until the pastor began making inappropriate comments to me.

"I'm attracted to your spirit, Allen," he said one day while we were meeting in his office. I think he was testing the waters to see how I'd respond. Those kinds of comments escalated over time to an overtly sexual proposition. Before I could get out of his office, he grabbed me, kissed my neck, and touched me inappropriately. I ran out of that church at the tender age of twenty-one, feeling betrayed and completely confused about what had just happened. *How could a man with a beautiful wife and two beautiful children and a church of two thousand people behave like this and get away with it?* I thought.

You might think that was the last time I set foot in that church, but it wasn't. I was right back there the next Sunday, still struggling to reconcile my faith with the disturbing things I was experiencing. Eventually I confronted the pastor about his same-sex attraction and asked about his thoughts on homosexuality. Using the Bible, he tried to convince me that homosexuality was not a sin as long as it was in the context of a loving, monogamous relationship. Thankfully I had never struggled with same-sex attraction, and since I was reading my Bible regularly at this point, I saw through his attempts to twist Scripture to justify his own behavior.

Although homosexuality and same-sex attraction are outside the scope of this book, the principle remains that when we're not grounded in proper doctrine, we're susceptible to false teachings that can derail our lives.

Years later, after I graduated from college, I finally found the courage to leave that church. I share this experience to illustrate how *easy* it is to be misled and how *hard* it can be to leave a church even when you know something is wrong. Looking back now, more than two decades later, it's obvious I was in an abusive relationship, but at the time I thought it was normal because it was all I knew. It wasn't until I broke free that I realized how toxic the environment was.

SHEEP WITHOUT A SHEPHERD

Mark 6:34 describes Jesus' heart for His generation: "When he went ashore, he saw a large crowd and had compassion on them, because they were like sheep without a shepherd. Then he began to teach them many things."

During Jesus' earthly ministry, His heart was overcome with compassion as He looked upon a generation of people who were lost and misguided. They were under the burdensome influence of many false teachers. Seeing the unnecessary bondage of that generation, Jesus compared them to sheep without a shepherd. His compassion moved Him to "teach them many things."

When I look at the body of Christ today and see so many of my brothers and sisters being misled, I feel the same kind of compassion. When I receive emails from people who are confused about the teaching they are receiving, it burdens me. When I read the comments on my YouTube channel from people who are being deceived and don't even know it, it cuts me straight to the heart—so much so that I've dedicated my life to helping people develop a solid Christian worldview.

It burdens me because I've been there. I know firsthand what it's like to be immersed in a church culture that you are convinced is teaching the truth but is misleading you, even harming you. I was blessed to break free after only a few years, but many don't. When I got out from under that false teaching, I made it my life's mission to help others find a way out too. It's my heart's desire that everyone who reads this book will be able to discern truth from error. I hope to save you from wasting precious years of your life under false teaching and manipulative leaders, and I want to equip you so you can help others do the same.

HOW TO READ THIS BOOK

I am a Bible teacher, so it's no surprise that this book is filled with Scripture. I know that's not too popular these days, but God's Word is what we need most. You don't need to know my opinion; you need to know what God says. As we begin this journey, I encourage you to grab your Bible, a highlighter, a pen, and a journal so you can write down the scriptures you encounter in this book. Study them on your own and test my words against God's Word. Look at each verse within the context of its full passage. Filling your heart and mind with Scripture, along with developing a vibrant prayer life, is the key for discerning when you're being guided toward truth and when you're being misled.

Throughout this book you'll read about a fictional character named Jarren on a journey to find a healthy, Bible-based church. He runs into false teachings that derail his life in one way or another. Each chapter begins with a story about Jarren's journey that illustrates the danger of believing a particular false teaching. Some of these stories are completely fictional, while others are based on my own experience or the experiences of people I've observed during twenty-five years of ministry. I'll let you figure out which is which!

Following each story is a detailed explanation of the false teaching Jarren encountered so you can identify it for yourself. We then analyze that teaching against the backdrop of Scripture to demonstrate why it's false. We'll also discuss why each false teaching is dangerous to individual believers and, most importantly, how it threatens the purity of the gospel of Jesus Christ. In their own way, these false teachings are a perversion of the gospel and must be rejected. Finally, each chapter will conclude with practical advice about what to look for so you can avoid being misled.

It's my sincere hope and prayer that you would read this book with an open mind and that it will inspire you to turn to the life-giving truth of God's Word whenever false teachings threaten to mislead you.

ONE

I HAVEN'T SPOKEN IN TONGUES. AM I MISSING OUT?

Now this is the type of church I can see myself attending! For the first time in his life, Jarren felt at home during a church service. The energy and atmosphere were electric, enhanced with carefully timed lighting. The music was upbeat. People were standing and shouting and singing loudly, hands waving or held palms-up in prayer. The preacher spoke with passion and conviction. Jarren's emotions—his entire being—felt stirred by it all.

This was a new experience for him, after growing up in a church where no one dared to say "Amen!"—even when the pastor was preaching his heart out. At that church the music leader called out a page number from the traditional hymnal, the congregation stood to sing, and then everyone sat down as the final organ notes faded.

When Jarren went off to college, he vowed to never again sit through a boring church service. And attending church was the furthest thing from his mind until his sophomore year, when a friend on campus named Ethan invited him to a service. Jarren was more than skeptical. *I bet this church is just like the one I grew up in. Boring. Dry. Irrelevant. A complete waste of time.* But Ethan kept pestering him to come, assuring him that *this* church was unlike anything he'd ever experienced.

Against his better judgment, Jarren agreed to go—and was blown away by the joy, passion, and excitement he experienced. That first visit soon turned into regular weekly attendance, and before long Jarren began anticipating Sunday mornings.

But one week he encountered something at Tongues of Fire Fellowship that he wasn't equipped to handle. In the middle of the worship experience, the worship leader started speaking in what sounded like a different language. Jarren assumed he must be bilingual. Glancing around the congregation, he wondered which attendees spoke that language. *It doesn't sound like any language I've ever heard before.* He shifted his weight and hid his awkwardness, as no one else appeared surprised or confused by this new development.

Then later in the service, in the middle of the sermon, the pastor also began to speak in an unusual-sounding language. *Who is he speaking to?* Jarren wondered. After about a minute, a wave of people around Jarren began to join in speaking the language, their voices overlapping in a growing, energetic wave. His heart sped up and he felt his body tense as his discomfort and confusion increased. The church that had quickly become like home suddenly felt strange and unsettling.

After the service Jarren pulled Ethan aside. "Bro! You're gonna have to explain that. What in the world just happened in there?"

"That's called speaking in tongues," Ethan said. Seeing Jarren's furrowed brow and uncertain expression, he smiled and patted Jarren's shoulder. "That's when you speak to God and others in a language you've never learned before. It's something you *must* do if you want to experience all that God has for you. Without this gift from the Holy Spirit, you'll be limited. You won't walk in the full power that God intends for you. Honestly, it's the first sign that you really are saved and have the Holy Spirit inside of you."

What? Jarren felt total confusion and shock. *I thought I was already saved. I thought I already have the Holy Spirit inside me.* Now his understanding of the Holy Spirit and the requirements to be a Christian were being challenged. It's as if he'd found a loose thread in the tapestry of his religious beliefs, and the more he pulled on it the more everything seemed to unravel.

In the next few months Jarren questioned absolutely everything he had once believed about God and salvation. He became obsessed with experiencing this gift and power of the Spirit. Church leaders noticed his efforts and offered counsel and coaching about how to experience the gift of tongues for himself. At first Jarren appreciated the care and attention. But as weeks passed and he still hadn't received the gift of tongues, the church leaders and fellow attendees began to express disappointment, frustration, and even judgment. The joyful sense of belonging Jarren had initially felt disappeared. He began to feel like a second-rate Christian and eventually left the church.

WHAT IS THE GIFT OF TONGUES?

Jarren's experience is not uncommon. Speaking in tongues is one of the most hotly debated topics within Christianity today. It's so divisive that some Christians have even broken fellowship with others who don't share their beliefs. In this chapter we'll identify false beliefs about the gift of tongues that are responsible for misleading so many well-meaning Christians, including those who've had experiences like Jarren's. But first let's look at exactly what this gift is according to the Scriptures.

Subsequent to Jesus' resurrection and preceding His ascension, He promised the arrival of a Comforter, the Holy Spirit, who would empower the disciples: "You will receive power when the Holy Spirit has come on you, and you will be my witnesses in Jerusalem, in all Judea and Samaria, and to the ends of the earth" (Acts 1:8).

Just days after Jesus ascended to heaven, His promise about the Holy Spirit's arrival and empowering work was fulfilled in supernatural fashion. But before we dig into that event, some context is necessary. Jewish males were required to make three annual pilgrimages to the holy city of Jerusalem to celebrate different Jewish feasts. Three times a year Jerusalem was filled with Jewish people from various countries, who spoke a multitude of languages. They all gathered to celebrate Pentecost, also known as the Feast of Weeks (Leviticus 23:15–21). This multilingual gathering was the vital context for Acts 2:1–4:

> When the day of Pentecost had arrived, they were all together in one place. Suddenly a sound like that of a violent rushing wind came from heaven, and it filled the whole house where they were staying. They saw tongues like flames of fire that separated and rested on each one of them. Then they were all filled with the Holy Spirit and began to speak in different tongues, as the Spirit enabled them.

The Greek word translated "tongues" in verse 4 is *glossa*, from which we get our English word *glossary*. One possible translation of this Greek word could be "an utterance outside the normal patterns of intelligible speech and therefore requiring special interpretation, ecstatic language, ecstatic speech."[1]

If that's the intended meaning of *glossa* in this passage, it's quite possible that these men were speaking gibberish. But the exact nature of the miracle is clarified in verses 5–6: "Now there were Jews staying in Jerusalem, devout people from every nation under heaven. When this sound occurred, a crowd came together and was confused because each one heard them speaking in his own language." Regardless of the words these men were speaking, the people who were there *heard* in their own languages what the apostles said. The Greek word used for "language" in verse 6 is *dialekto*, which simply means "language of a nation or a region."[2]

We can unequivocally conclude that the original gift of tongues was all about the communication of God's truth. Either the speaker was granted the ability to speak in a language they had never learned or the hearers were able to understand what the speaker was saying in *their own native language,* regardless of the language the speaker was using.

Here's an illustration. Suppose I were to travel to Japan, and while there, God enabled me through the power of the Holy Spirit to speak Japanese, a language I've never learned. Or perhaps I just started speaking in some ecstatic language that no one on earth could understand because it wasn't an actual dialect—but miraculously, those listening to me were able to understand the gospel as if I were speaking Japanese to them, even though I never learned a single word of Japanese in my life. *That* would be a miracle that mirrors the account in Acts!

Some believe that speaking in tongues can also involve the ability to pray, praise, give thanks, or communicate with God in a heavenly language that no man or woman could ever understand (1 Corinthians 14:2). It is not within the scope of this book to debate whether or not this type of tongues is still active today. Suffice to say that tongues is a good gift intended to build up the church (verses 22, 26) and help Christians share the gospel (Acts 2). But there are some false beliefs about tongues, prevalent even among well-meaning, sincere Christians, that are dangerously misleading. At worst, these false beliefs can have a negative impact on a believer's ability to understand and experience the full joy of the gospel. Let's take a look.

FALSE BELIEF #1: YOU MUST SPEAK IN TONGUES TO BE SAVED

This is the first lie we must tear down. The reason why this belief is dangerous is because it is a direct threat to the gospel of Jesus Christ. Again and again in Scripture the way of salvation is made clear.

Ephesians 2:8–9 states, "You are saved by grace through faith, and this is not from yourselves; it is God's gift—not from works, so that no one can boast."

Look at how many phrases the apostle Paul used to get his point across that salvation is not rooted in anything we do. We are saved by *grace*, which means "unearned or unmerited favor."[3] There is nothing we can do to earn or deserve God's favor. Second, he said that salvation is "not from yourselves." We don't contribute to our salvation in any way. Our salvation did not originate from us. Third, he said that "it is God's gift." When we give gifts to people, we don't do it because they deserve it; we give from the kindness of our hearts. Fourth, Paul said that salvation is "not from works." And finally, he added the words "so that no one can boast." No one will be in heaven one day saying, "I figured out how to speak in tongues and because of that (along with what Jesus has done), I'm saved." No one will be able to boast about any works regarding their salvation.

> There is nothing we can do to earn or deserve God's favor.

If someone suggests that you must speak in tongues to be saved, they are guilty of adding a work of the believer to the finished work of Jesus on the cross. Any suggestion that the work Jesus did on the cross to save us is not sufficient and requires additional action on our part is dangerous and even heretical. Anyone who teaches that speaking in tongues is vital for salvation is teaching a perverted version of the gospel. And the danger this false teaching poses to those who buy into it is clear: those who receive this gift of speaking in tongues may find themselves putting confidence in their own works and spiritual status rather than in Christ alone. And any believers who, like Jarren, don't have this experience will start to question the validity of their salvation.

FALSE BELIEF #2: SPEAKING IN TONGUES IS THE INITIAL EVIDENCE OF THE HOLY SPIRIT

The false belief that speaking in tongues is a *condition* for salvation crops up in plenty of churches, but I've found that it's not the most common false teaching related to speaking in tongues. Maybe that's because it's so obviously contrary to Scripture. A much more common belief within certain Christian circles is the idea that you may be saved, but until you speak in tongues, you don't possess the Holy Spirit. Speaking in tongues is seen as the *initial evidence* that the Holy Spirit has been poured out on a believer. The problem with this view lies with the word *the*. In the early church, speaking in tongues was *an* evidence of the Holy Spirit's presence or indwelling but not the *initial* or *only* evidence. Those promoting this view neglect what most of the New Testament teaches about the evidence and ministry of the Holy Spirit in the life of a believer. Let's review key scriptural teachings about the Holy Spirit.

The Holy Spirit Indwells

One of the primary ministries of the Holy Spirit is to take up full residence within every believer. "Don't you know that your body is a temple of the Holy Spirit who is in you, whom you have from God? You are not your own" (1 Corinthians 6:19).

This idea is so familiar that we take it for granted, but for first-century believers it was a big deal. Up to that point it was understood that the Holy Spirit would come upon or fill a person to empower them for a certain task, but He would not permanently indwell that person. Consider the example of King

> One of the primary ministries of the Holy Spirit is to take up full residence within every believer.

9

Saul: "When Saul and his servant arrived at Gibeah, a group of prophets met him. Then the Spirit of God came powerfully on him, and he prophesied along with them. Everyone who knew him previously and saw him prophesy with the prophets asked each other, 'What has happened to the son of Kish? Is Saul also among the prophets?'" (1 Samuel 10:10–11).

The Holy Spirit briefly enabled Saul to prophesy but did not dwell permanently in him, as subsequent passages make clear (1 Samuel 16:14). Other examples of people who received the temporary empowerment of the Holy Spirit include Gideon (Judges 6:34), Samson (Judges 13:25), and Azariah (2 Chronicles 15:1).

The permanent indwelling of the Spirit is unique to New Testament believers. Jesus made this clear when He said, "I will ask the Father, and he will give you another Counselor to be with you forever" (John 14:16). Paul confirmed that this indwelling of the Spirit occurs at the moment of conversion: "In him you also were sealed with the promised Holy Spirit when you heard the word of truth, the gospel of your salvation, and when you believed" (Ephesians 1:13).

Notice this verse says nothing about the believer having to *do* anything upon conversion to receive the Holy Spirit. He is the down payment from God for our eternal inheritance because of Christ's finished work on the cross.

The Holy Spirit Guides

Another manifestation or ministry of the Spirit is His guidance. Jesus promised that the Holy Spirit would lead us and guide us, revealing that as we go through the Christian life, the Holy Spirit comes alongside us to show the will and ways of God: "When the Spirit of truth comes, he will guide you into all the truth. For he will not speak on his own, but he will speak whatever he hears. He will also declare to you what is to come" (John 16:13).

If you've ever heard a still, small voice within that prompted you to make a decision consistent with the will of God, you've experienced the guiding ministry of the Spirit.

The Holy Spirit Empowers

You may recall the promise Jesus gave His disciples in Acts 1:8, where He promised that they would receive power to do things they would not normally be able to do in their own strength. This promise remains for believers today.

The Holy Spirit also distributes at least one spiritual gift to every believer: "A manifestation of the Spirit is given to each person for the common good" (1 Corinthians 12:7). But the Holy Spirit not only *distributes* these gifts to every believer; He also *empowers* us to use them. "All these are empowered by one and the same Spirit, who apportions to each one individually as he wills" (1 Corinthians 12:11 ESV).

If you've ever felt insecure or inadequate about using your spiritual gift or sharing your faith, only to discover in yourself a previously unimagined boldness or ability, you've experienced the empowering ministry of the Spirit.

The Holy Spirit Teaches

One of the most common ministries of the Holy Spirit is to teach us the truth of God's Word and remind us of these truths at the appropriate time. As Jesus said, "The Counselor, the Holy Spirit, whom the Father will send in my name, will teach you all things and remind you of everything I have told you" (John 14:26).

When we don't understand something pertaining to our faith, we can trust the Holy Spirit to teach it to us. Granted, our ability to hear from the Holy Spirit may be flawed. For this reason God has blessed the body of Christ with gifted theologians and scholars to teach the

Bible to others. But guess who taught it to them? The Holy Spirit. Whether directly or indirectly, the Spirit is actively teaching all God's people and reminding them of the words of Jesus.

The Holy Spirit Fills

The filling of the Spirit is something believers experience on a regular basis as a part of their Christian life. Look at Paul's command to believers: "Don't get drunk with wine, which leads to reckless living, but be filled by the Spirit" (Ephesians 5:18).

When we are intoxicated, we're under the influence or control of another substance. Here Paul commands that we allow ourselves to be influenced, or controlled, by the Holy Spirit instead of any physical or chemical substance. At times we may not be filled by the Holy Spirit, but we have already established that believers never lose the *indwelling* of the Spirit. So what is the difference between the filling and the indwelling of the Spirit? Several pastors and theologians have described the difference this way: The indwelling of the Spirit is when He becomes a *resident*, but the filling of the Spirit is when He becomes the *president*.[4] He will always be a resident, but it's up to us to allow Him to be the president of our lives.

The Holy Spirit Produces Fruit

Perhaps the most visible ministry of the Holy Spirit is producing fruit in a believer's life. The apostle Paul famously identified this "fruit of the Spirit" as "love, joy, peace, patience, kindness, goodness, faithfulness, gentleness, and self-control," then added, "The law is not against such things" (Galatians 5:22–23).

When we are tempted to be unloving, the Spirit helps us love. When we are tempted to be impatient toward people, the Spirit enables us to exercise patience instead. When we are tempted to yield to the sinful desires of our flesh, the Spirit enables us to exercise self-control.

Given the scope of the Spirit's work revealed in Scripture, we cannot isolate one activity of the Spirit—namely, speaking in tongues—as the *only* evidence of the Holy Spirit's indwelling or presence. The Bible is crystal clear that the Holy Spirit manifests Himself in a variety of ways in a believer's life. If a believer experiences *any* of the ministries of the Holy Spirit, that is proof of His residence, or presence, in the believer's life. But none of these ministries are *conditions* for receiving the Spirit. The Spirit is a gift we receive at the moment of conversion, apart from anything we could ever do.

FALSE BELIEF #3: THE BOOK OF ACTS PROVES THAT BELIEVERS MUST WAIT FOR THE BAPTISM OF THE SPIRIT

Some point to specific passages in the book of Acts as proof that speaking in tongues is an essential experience for every believer subsequent to salvation. This view is similar to the false beliefs about speaking in tongues being essential to salvation or being the initial sign of the Spirit's indwelling. However, the idea here is that the baptism of the Spirit, which manifests through speaking in tongues, is a distinct experience that awaits all Christians sometime *after* salvation. Here is one of the primary passages that proponents of this belief point to:

While Apollos was in Corinth, Paul traveled through the interior regions and came to Ephesus. He found some disciples and asked them, "Did you receive the Holy Spirit when you believed?"

"No," they told him, "we haven't even heard that there is a Holy Spirit."

"Into what then were you baptized?" he asked them.

"Into John's baptism," they replied.

Paul said, "John baptized with a baptism of repentance, telling the people that they should believe in the one who would come after him, that is, in Jesus."

When they heard this, they were baptized into the name of the Lord Jesus. And when Paul had laid his hands on them, the Holy Spirit came on them, and they began to speak in tongues and to prophesy.

—Acts 19:1–6

There is a *lot* to unpack here! Many from charismatic circles use this passage of Scripture as proof that there could be a time gap between genuine conversion and receiving the Spirit. Because of this isolated story, they conclude that it's possible for someone to be a Christian and not yet have the Holy Spirit. And based on how this narrative unfolds, they claim that speaking in tongues provides clear evidence that someone has received the Holy Spirit (again, sometime after genuine conversion).

The first mistake proponents of this view make is using a specific experience in a narrative book as the foundation for a normative doctrine for believers to follow today. In other words, they mistakenly identify as *prescriptive* a part of Scripture that is merely *descriptive*. The Bible is the unified Word of God, but it's also a complex collection of many different genres, including historical narrative, poetry, letters, and prophetic works. The book of Acts is primarily a historical narrative *describing* the various experiences of believers in the early church as the Holy Spirit enabled the initial spread of the gospel. It is not necessarily *prescribing* that readers repeat or follow whatever the narrative describes. The big problem with making the events of Acts 19:1–6 normative is that it was not consistent or normative even in the early church! For example, on the day of Pentecost, three thousand people were saved—but there is no mention of anyone speaking in tongues (Acts 2:41).

The second major mistake is that this view clearly contradicts New Testament teaching regarding when a believer receives the Spirit: "You, however, are not in the flesh, but in the Spirit, if indeed the Spirit of God lives in you. If anyone does not have the Spirit of Christ, he does not belong to him" (Romans 8:9). Here Paul made it unequivocally clear that if someone does *not* have the Spirit, they are not a Christian.

So what does all this mean for our interpretation of Acts 19:1–6? Notice how Paul phrased the question: "Did you receive the Holy Spirit when you believed?" The implication is clear: the Spirit takes up residence at the moment one believes, and if these people hadn't even heard of the Spirit, they were not Christians. The text strongly suggests they were John the Baptist's disciples but not yet believers in Jesus. They had embraced John's preparatory message of repentance from sin, but they had yet to experience true conversion to Jesus. John's ministry prepared the way for Jesus' ministry, but it wasn't the full gospel.

The disciples described in Acts 19 were equivalent to Old Testament saints in need of genuine conversion by believing in the name of Jesus for the remission of their sins. Once the true gospel was communicated to them and they believed, the Spirit entered them and they began speaking in tongues.

Now, listen carefully! God decided to give *this particular group* the evidence and assurance of the Holy Spirit's presence in their lives through speaking in tongues. But as we've already seen, this experience isn't normative for all Christians.

The reality is that in most of the conversion stories in the book of Acts, a genuine conversion experience was *not* accompanied by speaking in tongues (e.g., Acts 8:26–40; 9:1–19; 13:44–52; 16:11–15, 25–34; 17:1–10a, 10b–15, 16–33; 18:1–11, 24–28). Why would we make normative the few instances where tongues immediately followed salvation?

FALSE BELIEF #4: EVERY CHRISTIAN CAN AND SHOULD SPEAK IN TONGUES

A softer and less specific—but no less dangerous—false belief that is promoted by some of our charismatic brothers and sisters is the idea that every Christian can and should speak in tongues. The timing and significance isn't their focus, but they exert significant pressure on believers to continually seek this experience subsequent to salvation.

Those who espouse this view often convince people that *every* believer has the ability to speak in tongues, and if each believer exercises enough faith, they will bring this dormant gift to life. The implication is that if someone doesn't take advantage of this hidden treasure that's available to all believers, the fault is theirs. This needlessly saddles young believers with embarrassment, insecurity, and even shame when they don't speak in tongues.

This teaching is inconsistent with Scripture. We must remember that Scripture cannot contradict itself. Let's look at one clear passage from 1 Corinthians: "One and the same Spirit is active in all these, distributing to each person as he wills" (12:11). Scholars universally agree that 1 Corinthians is not a narrative like the book of Acts but rather a doctrinal book intended for the church to follow.

> The Holy Spirit decides who gets which gifts.

Notice who is in control of giving spiritual gifts. Can believers pick and choose which gifts they receive? No. The Holy Spirit decides who gets which gifts. A few verses later Paul asked, "Are all apostles? Are all prophets? Are all teachers? Do all do miracles? Do all have gifts of healing? Do all speak in tongues? Do all interpret? But desire the greater gifts. And I will show you an even better way" (1 Corinthians 12:29–31).

Paul's questions in this passage are clearly rhetorical. Obviously not every believer is an apostle. Obviously not every believer is a prophet. Obviously not every believer is gifted to teach the Bible. Obviously not every believer is able to do miracles. Obviously not every believer is able to heal sick people at will. So if it is obvious that not every believer would have all these gifts, why would we assume that every believer should be able to speak or pray in tongues?

Some will point to 1 Corinthians 14:5, where Paul said, "I wish all of you spoke in tongues, but even more that you prophesied. The person who prophesies is greater than the person who speaks in tongues, unless he interprets so that the church may be built up." If Paul wished that everyone spoke in tongues, doesn't that imply that every Christian *can* and *should*? Not necessarily. In fact, a careful comparison of similar scriptures suggests just the opposite. Consider Paul's comments about marriage and singleness earlier in this same letter to the Corinthian church: "I wish that all people were as I am. But each has his own gift from God, one person has this gift, another has that" (1 Corinthians 7:7).

Paul was simply stating his desire—and he did this to make a point, not to lay down a universal, timeless norm for all Christians. He said that he wished every Christian had the ability to be single so they would be less distracted by marital concerns and more devoted in spreading the gospel. But he knew that wasn't possible. Why? His conclusion was that the ability to abstain from sex (and set aside the many gifts and responsibilities of married life) is a *gift* very few people possess. So we should interpret this not as a command or even a possibility that every Christian should try to live up to, but as a desire of Paul's that reflects his passion and commitment to spreading the gospel. In the same way, his comment about wishing that everyone could speak in tongues emphasizes his passion for evangelism. Paul could say, "I wish every Christian could speak in multiple languages to spread the gospel" while also recognizing (and teaching clearly in other passages) that the Spirit gives different gifts to different believers.

Mark 16:17–18 is another passage that's sometimes used as evidence that every Christian can speak in tongues. Let's take a look: "These signs will accompany those who believe: In my name they will drive out demons; they will speak in new tongues; they will pick up snakes; if they should drink anything deadly, it will not harm them; they will lay hands on the sick, and they will get well."

There are two problems with using this passage of Scripture to support the view that speaking in tongues is available to every believer. First, it is widely accepted that this passage wasn't found in the earliest and most reliable manuscripts. Study Bibles include a footnote shortly after verse 8 explaining that this passage was likely not part of Mark's original gospel and was added to the text by a scribe.

But let's assume for the sake of argument that this passage should be included in the canon of Scripture. We now run into a *bigger* issue. The passage states that "those who believe" will be given *five* supernatural abilities: they will be empowered to drive out demons, speak in new tongues, pick up deadly snakes, drink *anything* deadly, and heal the sick. Exegetically, you cannot extract one of these supernatural abilities and say that all believers will experience that ability but not the other four.

Clearly, not all Christians who speak in tongues have the power to drive out demons or walk into a hospital room and heal the sick. And I think you'd be hard-pressed to find someone who speaks in tongues who would be bold enough to drink a bottle of bleach or handle poisonous snakes to prove that God will protect them from dying. Sadly, some have taken this verse literally and have experienced harm.

The reality is that even if this passage was included in the original Scriptures, it merely states that a select group of believers will be given some amazing supernatural abilities that will validate their *ministry* so that people will be more willing to listen to their *message*. But this is not a promise for all believers.

FALSE BELIEF #5: CHRISTIANS CAN PRAY IN TONGUES IN FRONT OF OTHERS WITH NO INTERPRETATION

In 1 Corinthians 14 Paul provided clear guidelines for how the gift of tongues should be used in a church context. First he shared his own perspective: "I thank God that I speak in tongues more than all of you; yet in the church I would rather speak five words with my understanding, in order to teach others also, than ten thousand words in a tongue. Brothers and sisters, don't be childish in your thinking, but be infants in regard to evil and adult in your thinking" (1 Corinthians 14:18–20).

Paul was thankful that he had been given the ability to speak in tongues, but he emphasized the value of speaking words that other people could understand. In verse 20 he even implied that to do otherwise is spiritual immaturity. Then he laid down this principle for the entire church:

> If, therefore, the whole church assembles together and all are speaking in tongues and people who are outsiders or unbelievers come in, will they not say that you are out of your minds? But if all are prophesying and some unbeliever or outsider comes in, he is convicted by all and is called to account by all. The secrets of his heart will be revealed, and as a result he will fall facedown and worship God, proclaiming, "God is really among you."
>
> —1 CORINTHIANS 14:23–25

Paul's focus was on the health of the church, and he was especially concerned about two groups of people: *unbelievers* and the *uninformed*.

He said that if the uninformed come to church and witness people speaking in tongues with no interpretation, they will conclude that the people are out of their minds. If they are unbelievers, they will be even more convinced that this church is some sort of a crazy house or cult where people are speaking in some secret language that only they know. In short, Paul was concerned that speaking in tongues without any sort of interpretation would lead to confusion and be completely ineffective for guiding people toward saving faith. But he had a solution:

> What then, brothers and sisters? Whenever you come together, each one has a hymn, a teaching, a revelation, a tongue, or an interpretation. Everything is to be done for building up. If anyone speaks in a tongue, there are to be only two, or at the most three, each in turn, and let someone interpret. But if there is no interpreter, that person is to keep silent in the church and speak to himself and God.
>
> —1 CORINTHIANS 14:26–28

Notice that Paul didn't forbid tongues. Instead he set guidelines to maintain order. Only two or three believers should take turns speaking in tongues, and there must be an interpreter at all times. This isn't what we see in many charismatic churches today. Instead we see hundreds, even thousands, of believers speaking in tongues at the same time with no interpretation. At times we even see lead pastors speaking in tongues from the pulpit and encouraging their members to do so with no interpretation. This is a clear disregard for Scripture.

Why is this happening? There are two common justifications. The first is a supposed distinction between *praying* in tongues and *speaking* in tongues. Many suggest that Paul's instructions prohibited *speaking* in tongues during a church service without an interpreter but didn't restrict *praying* in tongues, even if no interpreter is present. Now how ridiculous is that in light of Paul's teaching on the subject?

Do we honestly think that an unbeliever would enter a church service with absolutely no context for Christianity or the gift of tongues and be able to distinguish between someone speaking in tongues and praying in tongues? Either way unbelievers would be confused and come to the same conclusion: "This is craziness!" Then they would make a beeline for the door and never come back.

The second justification for disregarding Paul's instructions is that when people are speaking in tongues, they aren't in control of themselves; the power of the Spirit has overtaken them. This is a somewhat frightening justification, but we can disprove it as easily as the first. One of the biggest mistakes many Christians make is to elevate their experience above Scripture. You'll even hear some Christians say, "Well, I don't care what the Bible says. I know what I experienced."

God forbid you ever say that! Just think about it for a second. Is it possible for the same Holy Spirit who inspired Paul to give these instructions to also cause you to speak or pray in tongues in church without an interpreter present and create confusion and disorder? The Spirit in you would be contradicting the Spirit in Paul. This is contrary to the clear teaching of Scripture.

After wrapping up instructions for orderly worship in the areas of tongues and prophecy, Paul wrote, "Remember that people who prophesy are in control of their spirit and can take turns. For God is not a God of disorder but of peace, as in all the meetings of God's holy people" (1 Corinthians 14:32 NLT).

God's intent is not for believers to be so out of control that they are unable to govern their actions during a service. So don't be misled if you walk into a service where people are speaking in tongues without an interpreter. This is a violation of Scripture, and you should immediately leave. If those people are willing to overlook something so basic and obvious regarding order in the church, they most likely are overlooking other important doctrines as well.

THE REAL PROBLEM

The major problem we face with this divisive issue of tongues is that it separates Christians into two classes: the *haves* and the *have-nots*. If you are in the former group, you are more spiritual than those in the latter group, leaving those in the latter group to feel inferior and insecure—or maybe even concerned that they're not really Christians at all, despite having put their faith in Jesus. Compounding their guilt is the belief that it's their fault they don't have this gift, since they've been taught it's accessible and available to all true believers.

> The divisive issue of tongues separates Christians into two classes: the *haves* and the *have-nots*.

This leads to another major problem: The have-nots are tempted to covet the gifts of the haves rather than being content with what God has given them. They can become preoccupied with obtaining a gift that may not be for them instead of focusing on using the gifts they have been given.

A HEALTHY BALANCE

So what have we learned in our study of the Holy Spirit and the gift of tongues? First, the Holy Spirit is given to believers as a permanent gift at the moment of conversion through faith in Christ. To suggest that a believer needs to seek a second experience, or baptism of the Holy Spirit, to complete or confirm their salvation is a perversion of the gospel and the finished work of Christ on the cross. Second, speaking in tongues is not the *initial* or *only* evidence of the presence of the Holy Spirit in a believer's life. The Holy Spirit can manifest His presence in our lives in multiple ways. Finally, not every believer has the ability to speak or pray in tongues. If this gift is still active today, which is hotly debated in certain circles, it is certainly not something promised to every believer. We must treat it like any other spiritual gift.

If you possess the ability to speak in tongues or pray to God in an unknown tongue, exercise that gift freely within the parameters set by Scripture. But don't make the mistake of pushing your experiences onto others. Guard against adopting the mindset that you are some-how spiritually superior to those who don't speak or pray in tongues. Remember that the mark of a spiritually mature person is not the *gifts* of the Spirit but the *fruit* of the Spirit.

My final advice is to seek unity, not division, in the body of Christ. Speaking in tongues is not a nonnegotiable of the Christian faith. It is a secondary issue and should not be the reason you break fellowship with Christians who believe differently than you do. But don't allow yourself to be misled! Hold on to the freedom of the true gospel, receive the gifts of the Holy Spirit with open hands, and take joy in the reality that God gives those gifts as He sees fit, for the purpose of encouraging and building up the church.

TWO

ARE HEALTH AND WEALTH GUARANTEED FOR ALL THE FAITHFUL?

ven though Jarren left his hypercharismatic church, he still craved
fellowship within an organized body of believers. He began to
search for a new church home, and before long he found an attractive possibility. Everyone at Abundance Fellowship was so welcoming,
the worship was expressive and free, and the sermons were very practical. Jarren left the services feeling encouraged. He even attended a
healing service and thought, *Wow! People can get healed simply by
being touched by a man!*

He was also intrigued by the new idea that God wanted him to be
wealthy. He had always struggled financially, with his expenses seeming
to just outpace his income and leaving him carrying a multitude of debts.

Soon after Jarren began regularly attending his new church, he
found out that his sister, Sarah, had been diagnosed with a rare form
of cancer. The doctors gave her only six months to live. When she
told him the prognosis over the phone, Jarren felt his world implode.
Invisible bricks crushed his chest. His immediate response was to ask
his new church family for support. As a young believer, all he knew to
do was pray and ask others to pray for Sarah.

After hearing about his sister, some of the church leaders took
Jarren aside, formed a circle, and began to pray for her. As they prayed,
he noticed that they weren't *asking* God to heal her; they were speaking
as if she was already healed.

"Lord, we thank you that right now Sarah is healed in the name of
Jesus!" they prayed.

This totally confused Jarren, because from what he could see, his
sister wasn't getting better. She was getting worse. After the prayer

he questioned the leaders. "Hey, I noticed that during the prayer you declared that my sister was already healed. Can we do that? I mean, how does that work when the doctors are saying she has only a few months to live?"

One of the leaders nodded. "Because of what Jesus has done for us, we have the right to declare total healing over her life. The Bible says that by His stripes we are healed!"

"Wait, what?" Jarren was more than a little confused. "If that's the case, then why do so many Christians die from sicknesses?"

"Great question!" one of the other pastors replied. "That's primarily because those people don't have enough faith to believe that God will heal them. God *wants* to heal them. They just need to believe by faith and receive it!"

Jarren was drawn to this idea—it seemed empowering. But he still had questions. "So, are you telling me that we can control what God does by our faith?"

The man shook his head. "Well, not exactly. It's more like this: God has already promised that we will be healthy based on what Jesus did for us on the cross. So when we pray in faith, we aren't really controlling God or manipulating Him to do something He doesn't already want to do for us. We are merely tapping into what God already wants to do and activating what is already ours. Does that make sense?"

"I think so," Jarren replied with a growing sense of excitement and hope. "Do you mean to tell me that if I have enough faith, God could heal my sister too?"

"Not could . . . *would*! He will heal her if you have enough faith. That's exactly how it works!"

Jarren was more than intrigued by now. "How do I know if I have enough faith? And how much faith is necessary for this kind of thing?"

"No one is really sure," the pastor replied. "But Jesus said if we had the faith of a mustard seed, we would move mountains. So probably not that much. When God sees our faith at a certain level, it activates His divine will to heal those who are sick."

Jarren felt as if a whole new world was opening up for him. He'd started the day filled with financial concerns and deep sadness about his sister and what looked like her losing battle with cancer. But now he was filled with hope. He left church convinced that God would heal Sarah. Over the next few months he prayed several times a day for Sarah's healing. He asked everyone he knew to join in praying for her. He even asked people on Facebook and Instagram. Everyone said that they would, but nothing seemed to change. If anything, Sarah's health continued to decline.

Eventually Jarren decided to muster up a few hundred dollars to fly his sister into town to visit his church. Maybe she needed people to physically lay hands on her so she could experience healing. After hearing about Jarren's church and how people were being healed, Sarah became hopeful and agreed it was worth a try. A few days later she joined Jarren for a Sunday morning service, and at Jarren's request, several key members of his church formed a circle around his sister to pray for her. They offered heartfelt prayers in faith for God to heal her. Once again, they declared that she was healed and spoke as if it was a done deal. When she flew home the next day, both she and Jarren were filled with renewed confidence that God would work a miracle.

Just a few days later on a Tuesday afternoon, he received a call from his mother.

"Are you sitting down?" she asked.

"Yes. You're scaring me. Is everything okay?"

"Jarren, I'm sorry. The doctors did all they could to save Sarah, but she's gone. She passed about fifteen minutes ago, and I wanted you to know."

"No, this can't be! I had everyone praying for her, and I just knew we all had enough faith for her to be healed." Jarren got off the phone with his mother and felt the pain swallow him as he began to cry. Days turned into months as he sank into a deep depression, angry with God and blaming himself (and God) for Sarah's death. Abundance Fellowship no longer felt like home, so he stopped attending. He was haunted by one thought day and night: *If only I had more faith, my sister would still be here with me today.*

WHAT IS THE PROSPERITY GOSPEL?

Churches that teach people to claim, tap into, declare, decree, or activate God's blessings of health and wealth are some of the fastest-growing churches in the world today. They attract—and mislead—many new believers like Jarren. They teach a false gospel called the *prosperity gospel*, which we'll explore and expose in this chapter.

Prosperity theology, the prosperity gospel, the Word of Faith movement, and health-and-wealth theology are all terms for this false doctrine. Together they comprise a collection of teachings that share a few common features, especially the notion that financial prosperity and perfect health are always the will of God for believers. Within this doctrine, health and wealth are two sides of the same coin. Anything short of experiencing these blessings means you are living outside of God's will for your life. Proponents of this view usually teach that physical health and financial prosperity are available to all believers because of the finished work of Jesus on the cross.

Robert Tilton, one of the prosperity gospel's well-known spokesmen, wrote, "I believe that it is the will of God for all to prosper because I see it in the Word, not because it has worked mightily for someone else. I do not put my eyes on men, but on God who gives me the power to get wealth."[1]

Putting our eyes on Scripture instead of our experiences is wise— but does the Bible really tell us that God's will is for all believers to become financially wealthy? Is that truly what the gospel is about? Consider the apostle Paul's warning: "Even if we or an angel from heaven should preach to you a gospel contrary to what we have preached to you, a curse be on him!" (Galatians 1:8).

The gospel preached by Paul couldn't be any clearer: the true gospel is about salvation from sin by grace through faith. According to Galatians 1:8, people who promote a different gospel are under a curse and will stand before God to give an account. So anytime we're talking about the gospel, we're in serious, high-stakes territory. We cannot afford to get it wrong. And I believe that the prosperity gospel is one of the most seductive and dangerous false gospels around.

In the first part of this chapter, we'll specifically explore some of the major theological problems with the prosperity gospel and how it perverts the true gospel. Then we'll look at how and why this false gospel is so dangerous for believers. Finally, we'll look at what the Bible actually says about suffering and prosperity so we can strike a biblically balanced view on the subject.

PROBLEM #1: THE PROSPERITY GOSPEL IS INCONSISTENT WITH THE MESSAGE OF THE BIBLE

When we look at what the Bible says about health and wealth, it paints a very different picture from what the prosperity preachers present. Let's first look at what the Bible says about health. Here's a popular verse that many Christians like to quote to suggest that the atoning work of Jesus includes a promise of perfect health: "He was wounded for our transgressions, He was bruised for our iniquities; The chastisement for our peace was upon Him, And by His stripes we are healed" (Isaiah 53:5 NKJV).

Let's key in on the phrase "by His stripes we are healed." Looking at this verse in its immediate context, it cannot refer just to *physical* healing on this side of heaven. The words surrounding it are all *spiritual* in nature—words such as *transgressions, iniquities,* and *peace* refer to a spiritual healing, not physical wellness.

Now, is physical healing ultimately part of the promise of the gospel for believers? Yes, it is. Absolutely. But there is no divine promise that physical healing must take place here on earth. Christians will be physically healed once and for all in heaven, where God finally puts an end to all the effects of sin. But this side of heaven? Physical sickness continues to be part of the world's brokenness, even for those who have put their faith in Jesus.

Let's expand on this point. Most of the uses of the Hebrew word for *heal* or *healed* in the book of Isaiah, and other prophetic books for that matter, speak of a spiritual healing, not a physical one. Here are a few scriptures to consider:

> The LORD will strike Egypt, striking and healing. Then they will turn to the LORD, and he will be receptive to their prayers and heal them.
>
> —ISAIAH 19:22

> Make the minds of these people dull; deafen their ears and blind their eyes; otherwise they might see with their eyes and hear with their ears, understand with their minds, turn back, and be healed.
>
> —ISAIAH 6:10

> Then shall your light break forth like the dawn, and your healing shall spring up speedily; your righteousness shall go before you; the glory of the LORD shall be your rear guard.
>
> —ISAIAH 58:8 ESV

In all these passages, God wants to do a work of spiritual restoration and healing. Nothing in the context suggests that immediate physical healing in this life is part of the gospel. We'll discuss exactly what the Bible says about sickness and suffering later in this chapter.

The idea that every Christian is already blessed with material prosperity—you just have to walk in it and receive it—is also inconsistent with the overall biblical message. If wealth were God's will for every believer, Jesus and the New Testament writers would not have spent so much time speaking of money's dangers. They would have spent more time speaking of the blessings of obtaining wealth. As a matter of fact, the New Testament stresses contentment more than the desire to accumulate more and more: "But godliness with contentment is great gain. For we brought nothing into the world, and we can take nothing out" (1 Timothy 6:6–7).

Jesus said that we should focus on storing up treasures in heaven rather than here on earth: "Don't store up for yourselves treasures on earth, where moth and rust destroy and where thieves break in and steal. But store up for yourselves treasures in heaven, where neither moth nor rust destroys, and where thieves don't break in and steal" (Matthew 6:19–20).

We'll take a much closer look at the theology of money and wealth later in this chapter, but it should already be clear that when it comes to material wealth, the tone and focus of the Bible are a far cry from the messages of prosperity preachers. Instead of celebrating the pursuit of financial gain, Jesus and the writers of Scripture frequently point out the pitfalls associated with wealth.

PROBLEM #2: PHYSICAL HEALING IS NOT ALWAYS CONTINGENT ON PEOPLE'S FAITH

I've heard so many prosperity gospel proponents imply or even outright claim that if someone isn't healed, it's because they didn't have enough faith. While Scripture frequently connects the experience of miraculous healing with personal faith, a careful examination of Jesus' healings proves that we shouldn't imagine some sort of vending-machine system where we can expect healing if we put in enough faith. Jesus' choice to heal people was not always contingent on or even related to the faith of the recipient.

For instance, Matthew 4:24 describes several people Jesus healed, and none of them were healed on the basis of their faith: "Then the news about him spread throughout Syria. So they brought to him all those who were afflicted, those suffering from various diseases and intense pains, the demon-possessed, the epileptics, and the paralytics. And he healed them." In Matthew 8:16 we see something similar: "When evening came, they brought to him many who were demon-possessed. He drove out the spirits with a word and healed all who were sick."

> We shouldn't imagine a vending-machine system where we expect healing if we put in enough faith.

In fact, there are only a few instances when the person's faith was mentioned in conjunction with their physical healing, and scholars debate as to whether Jesus was connecting their faith to their physical healing or their spiritual salvation:

The healing that these people experienced is expressed in Greek, by a form of the word *sozo*, which means "to preserve, rescue, save from death, or keep alive." Sometimes *sozo* refers to spiritual salvation, which is also linked to a person's faith. For example, when the penitent prostitute washed Jesus' feet with her tears, He told her much the same thing: "Your faith has saved you" (Luke 7:50; for other examples, see Mark 10:52 and Luke 17:19). When Jesus spoke of the faith of the woman with the issue of blood in Matthew 9, His healing was very likely more than physical; it was a spiritual healing as well, as she is told to "go in peace" (Mark 5:34).[2]

This article goes on to make another great point: In some instances, Jesus chose *not* to heal everyone who was present. Take, for example, the healing of the man at the pool of Bethesda (John 5:1–13). Multitudes of sick people were present, but Jesus chose to heal only one man that day. And that man didn't even know it was Jesus who had healed him until later.

PROBLEM #3: THE PROSPERITY GOSPEL ISN'T EVEN AN OPTION IN MOST PARTS OF THE WORLD

Prosperity preachers seek to convince people that embedded in the gospel is a hidden promise that every believer should be healthy and wealthy. A major problem with this is that the majority of the world is considered impoverished:

> The majority of the world population still lives in poverty: Every tenth person lives on less than $1.90 per day and two-thirds live on less than $10 per day. In rich countries a person is considered poor when she or he lives on less than $30 per day; if we rely on this poverty definition then we find that 85% of the world live in poverty.[3]

I'd say that not one prosperity preacher would consider living on ten dollars a day as being prosperous. Does this mean that 85 percent of the world is living in sin because they're not tapping into the full promise of the gospel message? It's impossible to maintain that every Christian living in an impoverished, third-world country is devoid of the requisite level of faith needed to live and walk in prosperity.

Paula White, a well-known prosperity preacher, said, "God is not magnified when you are broke, busted, or disgusted."[4] Imagine how that sounds to someone who is struggling financially. Is the good news of Jesus really supposed to make them believe they cannot and will not magnify God until they earn more money?

PROBLEM #4: THE PROSPERITY GOSPEL TEACHES A FALSE DEFINITION OF FAITH

One of the biggest problems with the prosperity-theology movement is that it has an erroneous view of faith. Essentially, prosperity preachers teach that God has this vault of physical and material blessings available for every believer. If you have the right faith, you can unlock an endless supply of blessings for your life.

Kenneth Copeland, a leader in the prosperity movement, defines faith this way: "Faith is a spiritual force, a spiritual energy, a spiritual power. It is this force of faith which makes the laws of the spirit world function. . . . There are certain laws governing prosperity revealed in God's Word. Faith causes them to function."[5]

Did you catch that? Copeland says that faith unlocks blessings and makes the laws of the spirit world function. Speaking of the fallacy of the prosperity gospel in their book *Health, Wealth & Happiness*, David W. Jones and Russell S. Woodbridge strip away the biblical-sounding veneer and expose what the prosperity gospel is really saying: "Faith is a magic formula that enables believers to obtain what they desire."[6]

I'm here to tell you that faith is not some magical force or feeling we can conjure up to manipulate God in heaven to do something that will benefit us! Faith means placing your trust in the person of Christ and the promises of God as revealed in the Word of God.

Some within the prosperity gospel camp, who could have been healed through modern medicine, have even rejected medical help because they were taught to expect healing to come through purely supernatural intervention. If they take medicine, they reason, it could be said that it was the medicine that healed them and not God, demonstrating a lack of faith in God's ability and will to heal.

PROBLEM #5: PROSPERITY THEOLOGY GETS THE TIMELINE WRONG

This is perhaps the greatest problem with the prosperity gospel: it includes physical healing and financial prosperity as part of what Jesus accomplished for us on the cross. Kenneth Copeland confirms this by saying, "The basic principle of the Christian life is to know that God put our sin, sickness, disease, sorrow, grief, and poverty on Jesus at Calvary."[7]

This gets dicey because the most effective lies tend to have truth mixed in and, in one sense, Copeland is correct. By believing in Jesus we will ultimately be free from all those things. The problem is that he and other prosperity teachers promise that these blessings will happen on this side of heaven! The reality is that we will not realize the fullness of this promise until we receive glorified bodies that are imperishable and designed for eternity. According to Scripture, Jesus' primary purpose for going to the cross was to atone for our sins. But when we add physical healing and financial prosperity to that purpose, we are guilty of perverting the gospel.

WHY IS THE PROSPERITY GOSPEL DANGEROUS?

Now that we better understand what the Bible says about this false doctrine, let's examine why believing in the health-and-wealth gospel is so dangerous for individual believers. Prosperity theology is so enticing because it preys on our two greatest desires. Every human wants to be *healthy* and *wealthy*.

Danger #1: It Weakens Our Faith in God

One of the biggest dangers with the prosperity gospel is that it ultimately makes God look bad. Let me illustrate: If a father promised his daughter something she had been begging him for, but he failed to deliver on that promise, what do you think would happen to that girl's trust in her father?

When people believe that God has promised them health and wealth, and yet they find that their reality is drastically different from that expectation, it makes God look untrustworthy. Anytime there is a gap between expectations and experience, the result is extreme disappointment and disillusionment. This is sadly what many Christians have experienced as a result of the prosperity gospel.

If we start to feel that God cannot be trusted, our faith in God begins to weaken. We no longer believe that God fulfills His promises. The fallacy here is obvious: if we believe that God will do something He has never promised, we can reach the point where we blame God for our pain and poverty.

Danger #2: It Creates False Guilt

By teaching people that God's will for believers is to be healthy and wealthy, the prosperity gospel saddles them with false guilt whenever there is a gap between their expectations and their experiences. The believer naturally begins to think, *I must be doing something wrong because I'm still struggling financially.* The easiest way for prosperity preachers to explain why some believers aren't experiencing the health and wealth they believe God has promised is to blame them, accusing them of not having enough faith to activate these blessings. This can and does create extreme psychological damage for the believer who fails to achieve health and wealth, as was the case with Jarren.

> If we start to feel God cannot be trusted, our faith in God begins to weaken.

Danger #3: It Creates False Hope

Prosperity theology teaches that when believers give sacrificially to the Lord, they can *hope* to receive a financial blessing in return. This is often called *seed sowing* (we'll discuss this later in the chapter). You may hear a prosperity preacher say something like, "Sow a seed into the work God is doing in this ministry and watch Him return it to you tenfold." Of course, the seed these preachers are asking for is money their listeners often cannot afford to give. These statements prey on the desperation of the giver for a quick solution to their financial problems, like winning the lottery. One of the most effective ways to keep people buying lottery tickets is showing the stories of people who have won in the past. Success stories keep the masses hoping they will be next. Prosperity theology uses many of the same tactics.

Danger #4: It Promises a Quick Fix to Problems

Leadership expert Stephen R. Covey has observed that "you can't talk your way out of a problem that you behaved your way into."[8] You could also say that you can't *believe* your way out of a problem you behaved your way into. Regarding debt and wealth, instead of only teaching people biblical principles for how to get out of debt, invest, start a business, and accumulate wealth over time, most prosperity preachers promise a tenfold or even a hundredfold blessing. Far from helping people with their financial troubles, these preachers distract people from applying basic wealth management principles by promising them a quick fix to problems.

Regarding health, a person's problems may be resolved through lifestyle choices or medical treatment. But instead of teaching the importance of a proper diet and exercise in improving health outcomes, prosperity preachers promise immediate and total healing.

Danger #5: It Steals God's Glory and Gives It to Man

While many prosperity preachers give glory to God when an alleged healing takes place, the reality is that many of their followers place their faith not in God but in those who claim to have healing power. This is why hundreds of thousands of people show up at healing crusades. They hope that a faith healer will call them onstage and immediately heal them with a touch. The sad assumption is that if they are not fortunate enough to be touched by a supposed faith healer, then they won't be healed. The glory in these situations is more focused on the alleged faith healer than on God, the ultimate Healer.

Danger #6: It Can Create a Transactional Relationship with God

Many prosperity preachers leverage all their eloquence, using Scripture of course, to convince their hearers that if they sow a seed into their ministry, God will bless them financially. Many well-meaning believers have fallen for this trap. Gloria Copeland, the wife of Kenneth Copeland, said, "Give $10 and receive $1,000; give $1,000 and receive $100,000. . . . In short, Mark 10:30 is a very good deal."[9]

This is one of the most dangerous effects of the prosperity gospel.

The story goes something like this: A believer needs a financial break-through. Perhaps they are in serious debt and believe God will provide them with money for what they want to do. Instead of applying biblical and commonsense principles to get out of debt or save money, they put their faith in a spiritual lottery system. A prosperity preacher convinces them that they will receive a financial reward for sowing into the preacher's ministry. So people give sacrificially by faith and wait for their financial breakthrough. But, sadly, that financial break-through doesn't come, and believers are left devastated and even more destitute than before.

It's time to examine what the Bible actually says about sowing and reaping. The basic principle is laid out for us in 2 Corinthians 9:6: "The point is this: The person who sows sparingly will also reap sparingly, and the person who sows generously will also reap generously." God never promises to bless us *financially* if we give financially. Sowing generously does lead to reaping generously, but God will bless us in whatever way *He* sees fit. The prosperity preachers seek to convince you that there is a direct return on your money, like an investment. If it were that simple, we'd have a whole lot more giving going on in the church—and a whole lot more millionaires as well!

Let's look at what some of the most popular prosperity preachers are saying about giving. Bishop T. D. Jakes said,

Remember, no need is too big for God. Maybe you need a miracle in your marriage. God can put it back together. You could be facing unbelievable financial challenges; God can provide a supernatural increase. God knows where you need your miracle harvest, and now is the time to sow your Miracle Faith Seed. Even if you've already shared a gift, you still have time to increase your blessing during this miracle season of sowing. Take a moment to do two things: First, write your most urgent prayer request on the reply form and send it to me so I may join you in praying for your miracle harvest! Second, take a moment to sow the most generous miracle faith seed you can.[10]

Whoa! Let's take a moment and unpack exactly what he's saying here. First, T. D. Jakes preys on people's desperation for a miracle by imploring them to sow a miracle faith seed. Then he mixes in some truth, assuring his listeners that God *can* "provide a supernatural increase." Yes, that's true. Next, he concludes that since they need a miracle harvest, the way to get that is to sow a miracle faith seed. Then he says they still have time to increase their blessing. The idea is that your ability to obtain more financial blessings depends on how much more you give. Finally he promises to join in praying for their miracle and encourages them to give the "most generous miracle faith seed" they can.

Another prosperity preacher named Jerry Savelle said, "Any time a worried thought about money pops up in your mind the next thing you do is sow.... Stop worrying, start sowing.... That's God's stimulus package for you."[11]

Once again, a preacher is setting forth a transactional relationship with God: give money to God so that He can give you even more right back! In an article about the prosperity gospel movement, David Jones observed, "Teachers of the prosperity gospel encourage their followers to pray, and even demand, of God 'everything from modes of transportation (cars, vans, trucks, even two-seat planes), homes, furniture, and large bank accounts.'"[12]

This give-to-get system is a perversion of giving. It is our *privilege* to give, and the main purpose of giving is to express our gratitude to the one who has already given us all that we need. But prosperity gospel teachers twist the meaning and purpose of giving, and in doing so they tempt people to give with the wrong motivation. In the give-to-get system, the expectation is somewhat like an investment. When we invest our money, we *expect* a certain percentage of return and will be disappointed or angry if we don't get it. No one invests money without expecting a return. The prosperity preachers teach people that they should never invest in God without expecting an increase. This is a dangerous doctrine because it strips believers of the joy and privilege of giving sacrificially from sincere hearts.

WHAT DOES THE BIBLE REALLY SAY ABOUT SUFFERING?

Now that we understand some of the dangers of prosperity theology, how can we come to a proper, balanced, and biblical understanding of health and wealth? Let's start with some context: namely, what the Bible tells us about suffering. Inherent in the prosperity gospel message is a promise to alleviate suffering in general—whether physical, emotional, financial, or otherwise.

In their preaching and teaching, advocates of the prosperity gospel speak in positive terms, focusing largely on economic prosperity, which is primarily a message of avoiding mental suffering because of finances. Another related theme is overcoming other types of suffering by flourishing in personal relationships, enjoying occupational success, and experiencing miraculous physical healings. Whether suffering is physical or mental, the prosperity gospel places great emphasis on avoiding it.[13]

Is this teaching consistent with Scripture? Far from it. Let's look at two biblical realities that stand against the prosperity gospel's attitude toward suffering.

Even the Faithful Suffer

Throughout the Bible we see examples of God's greatest servants enduring excruciating pain. Job endured unexplainable suffering. Joseph was thrown into a pit by his own brothers, sold into slavery, falsely accused of a crime, and unjustly imprisoned. David was persecuted by Saul. Hannah and many other women were barren for years, suffering the social stigma and emotional pain that went with being childless in the Jewish culture. Many of the Old Testament prophets were beaten, imprisoned, and killed for preaching the Word of God. Many of the apostles were martyred. Those who made it into the Hall of Faith in Hebrews 11 endured significant pain. And Jesus endured excruciating pain and suffering on the cross, which we know was the will of God.

Suffering Is Promised

Not only does the Bible depict people of faith enduring all kinds of suffering, but Jesus told His closest followers that they should *expect* to suffer. Take a look at these passages:

> "Remember the word I spoke to you: 'A servant is not greater than his master.' If they persecuted me, they will also persecute you. If they kept my word, they will also keep yours."
>
> —JOHN 15:20

> "I have told you these things so that in me you may have peace. You will have suffering in this world. Be courageous! I have conquered the world."
>
> —JOHN 16:33

The apostles also promised that suffering would be a part of this life, not just *despite* our faithfulness to Jesus, but *because* of it. Paul offered these warnings to early believers:

> It has been granted to you on Christ's behalf not only to believe in him, but also to suffer for him.
>
> —PHILIPPIANS 1:29

All who want to live a godly life in Christ Jesus will be persecuted.

—2 TIMOTHY 3:12

Paul wasn't talking about self-inflicted suffering arising from poor choices or bad habits. For instance, if I cheated on my wife and then endured a difficult divorce followed by the pain of being separated from my children, that entire season of suffering would be self-inflicted. But Paul was amplifying Jesus' warning: if the world hated and persecuted Jesus, we shouldn't be surprised when the world treats us as His followers the same way.

> We cannot expect to be exempt from suffering this side of the resurrection.

The New Testament is replete with scriptures affirming the presence of suffering in the life of the believer. If we're reading our Bibles with openness and honesty, we cannot expect to be exempt from suffering this side of the resurrection.

I consider that the sufferings of this present time are not worth comparing with the glory that is going to be revealed to us.

—ROMANS 8:18

In fact, all who want to live a godly life in Christ Jesus will be persecuted.

—2 TIMOTHY 3:12

Consider it a great joy, my brothers and sisters, whenever you experience various trials, because you know that the testing of your faith produces endurance. And let endurance have its full effect, so that you may be mature and complete, lacking nothing.

—JAMES 1:2–4

The God of all grace, who called you to his eternal glory in Christ, will himself restore, establish, strengthen, and support you after you have suffered a little while.

—1 PETER 5:10

Finally, look at Paul's vividly detailed explanation of how he suffered for preaching the gospel of Jesus:

Are they servants of Christ? I'm talking like a madman—I'm a better one: with far more labors, many more imprisonments, far worse beatings, many times near death. Five times I received the forty lashes minus one from the Jews. Three times I was beaten with rods. Once I received a stoning. Three times I was shipwrecked. I have spent a night and a day in the open sea.

—2 CORINTHIANS 11:23–25

The picture that the New Testament writers paint of the Christian life is vastly different from what the prosperity preachers are presenting.

WHAT ABOUT SICKNESS?

Not only is suffering part of the Christian life, but at times sickness can be as well. Let's examine four scenarios in the New Testament.

Paul's Thorn

In 2 Corinthians 12:7 Paul described a particular ailment he was dealing with: "So that I would not exalt myself, a thorn in the flesh was given to me, a messenger of Satan to torment me so that I would not exalt myself."

Scholars have long debated the nature of this thorn, since Paul doesn't give us any specifics. Assuming that it was a physical condition, the question remains, Why would God not heal, of all people, the great apostle Paul? And why did Paul not simply heal *himself* since he clearly had the gift of divine healing? Did Paul not have enough faith to believe God for his own healing? The context would suggest otherwise. Verse 8 says, "Concerning this, I pleaded with the Lord three times that it would leave me."

Paul's insistent pleading suggests that he had the faith to believe God could heal him. After all, he'd seen firsthand how God used him to heal others. Why would he not believe God could do the same for him? We can only conclude that for whatever reason God, in His divine wisdom, chose not to heal Paul. And if we can find one example of this, it proves that it cannot be God's will to heal everyone. But there are more examples.

Trophimus

Paul, writing from prison, described the difficulty of his situation, focusing especially on the fact that several of his closest partners in the ministry were not able to be with him in his time of need: "Only Luke is with me. Bring Mark with you, for he is useful to me in the ministry. . . . Erastus has remained at Corinth; I left Trophimus sick at Miletus" (2 Timothy 4:11, 20).

Assuming that Paul could have used Trophimus' aid while in prison, why did Paul not use his supernatural power to heal him? If perfect health was the norm for believers, it makes no sense for Paul to have left this man sick.

Timothy

A third example is someone much closer to Paul, a young man named Timothy. Paul considered Timothy his son in the ministry. This young man had a chronic stomach ailment and perhaps other health concerns. If there was anyone Paul would have healed, it would certainly have been Timothy. But notice the instructions Paul gave him instead. "Don't continue drinking only water, but use a little wine because of your stomach and your frequent illnesses" (1 Timothy 5:23).

If the expectation was that a believer could be healed at the hands of someone supernaturally gifted to do so, we would expect Paul to instruct Timothy to claim healing in the name of Jesus and meet with Paul or another apostle who could exercise this gift. This would have been a permanent fix rather than a temporary one. But the context suggests that Timothy's health problems would continue, and he would have to use Paul's recommended treatment on an ongoing basis. Notice that Paul didn't instruct Timothy to muster up enough faith to believe God for his healing. He didn't mention that Timothy had the authority to claim or expect healing. Nothing in this account suggests that physical health is normative for believers.

Epaphroditus

This is one example where the man was actually healed. But notice the details:

> I considered it necessary to send you Epaphroditus—my brother, coworker, and fellow soldier, as well as your messenger and minister to my need—since he has been longing for all of you and was distressed because you heard that he was sick. Indeed, he was so sick that he nearly died. However, God had mercy on him, and not only on him but also on me, so that I would not have sorrow upon sorrow.
>
> —Philippians 2:25–27

In Paul's account there is no mention of any faith healer working a miracle for Epaphroditus. Nor did Paul mention that Epaphroditus had a requisite level of faith or claimed healing as if it were some divine right he already possessed. No, Paul simply stated that "God had mercy on him." Apparently it was God's will for Epaphroditus to be healed. But the way Paul described the special mercy God showed in this situation reveals that healing isn't an outcome believers should expect or demand from God.

Despite these examples from the Word of God, health-and-wealth preachers continue to mislead people. Many respect and follow Joyce Meyer, and a number of her teachings are helpful and biblical. But she also teaches that you should recite certain affirmations over your life regarding healing, a practice rooted in prosperity theology. Consider her words:

> "I will" is the strongest assertion that can be made in the English language. God is speaking to me now saying, "I will take sickness away from the midst of thee." God is watching over this Word, performing it in me now. He is taking sickness away from the midst of me. Good-bye, sickness! The Lord is taking you away from the midst of me. Thank You, Father, for taking sickness away from me. I thank You for doing what You said. . . . I'm abiding under the shadow of Jehovah-Rapha, the Lord that healeth me. No plague shall come nigh my dwelling or my body. I resist sickness and disease. I refuse to accept it! It's not mine! I refuse to be sick in Jesus' Name. Sickness cannot trespass in my body. Sickness, (*name it*), you can't come nigh my dwelling. I refuse You! I resist you![14]

Do you see the danger in this teaching? Millions of people across the world believe that if they recite this affirmation, they'll somehow escape all sickness and disease. So when they or a loved one inevitably face illness, they are overwhelmed with concerns that their faith is too weak—or, worse yet, that God has abandoned them or failed to live up to His promises.

IS THE GIFT OF HEALING FOR TODAY?

Let's take a step back and look at the role of miracles in general. The first thing we must understand about miracle workers (including people with the gift of healing) is that they aren't as common as people may think, not even in the biblical narratives. A careful reading of the Bible reveals just three short periods in human history when miracles were prevalent. The first was during the time of Moses. God gave Moses the ability to perform miracles at will, such as turning his staff into a snake. The second time was hundreds of years later with Elijah and Elisha. They were given power from God to do things like calling down fire from heaven, keeping it from raining to cause a drought, healing the sick, and even raising the dead. Several hundred years after the time of Elijah and Elisha, Jesus and the apostles also performed an astonishing number of miracles.

What do all three of these time periods have in common? These were strategic, pivotal moments in salvation history when God was doing something new for His people. God gifted these particular men with the ability to perform miracles in order to authenticate their message. He knew that people wouldn't listen to their *message* without first seeing their *miracles*. The miracles were meant to convince onlookers that the men were messengers from God and worth listening to (though it didn't always work out that way).

> Miracle workers aren't as common as people may think.

Other than these three limited time periods, miracles and healings of the kind ascribed to Moses, Elijah, Elisha, Jesus, and the apostles do not seem to have been prevalent during any other point in history, including today. The supernatural ability to heal people or perform other miracles at will was granted during special moments to just a few people throughout all human history.

Today we don't see people walking around hospital wards healing people at will. Healings of that sort may have accompanied Jesus' ministry as well as the apostles' ministry as the church was being established. But what we tend to see today is that God, in His wisdom, grace, and sovereignty, listens to the prayers of His people and determines whom He will heal.

When we pray for God to heal someone, we don't demand that He do it. We aren't to claim supernatural healing as if it's already guaranteed. We don't pray as if God is obligated to do what we want. Rather, we humbly ask Him to extend mercy to our sick brother or sister, and we trust in His sovereign decision to heal or not to heal.

HOW SHOULD CHRISTIANS VIEW PROSPERITY?

For some strange reason, we have a tendency in the body of Christ to gravitate toward extremes. How Christians view money is no exception. On one hand, the prosperity gospel insists that every Christian should experience financial increase and that being wealthy is God's will for all who believe. We've discussed the dangers of this overemphasis on receiving financial blessings.

However, there is an error on the other side that we need to discuss: the glamorization of poverty, or what I like to call the poverty gospel. Some Christians see a lack of financial wealth as a badge of honor. Perhaps they believe that it shows their ultimate trust in God. Maybe they think that it proves to the outside world that money is not their idol. Maybe they fear that if they had financial wealth, people would question their integrity.

Since both extremes are damaging to the believer, I want to discuss what the Bible says about prosperity. To help us get a biblical perspective on money, we'll examine a couple of important passages in the book of 1 Timothy. The first is a warning about the dangers of becoming obsessed with wealth:

> If we have food and clothing, we will be content with these. But those who want to be rich fall into temptation, a trap, and many foolish and harmful desires, which plunge people into ruin and destruction. For the love of money is a root of all kinds of evil, and by craving it, some have wandered away from the faith and pierced themselves with many griefs.
>
> —1 TIMOTHY 6:8–10

This passage might give you the idea that accumulating wealth is evil. It says that we should be content with food and clothing, and if we want to be rich, we'll fall into temptation. It also says that the love of money causes people to wander away from the faith. All of these things are true. But notice that there is no outright ban on accumulating wealth. And if we keep on reading, we gain a balanced perspective:

> Instruct those who are rich in the present age not to be arrogant or to set their hope on the uncertainty of wealth, but on God, who richly provides us with all things to enjoy. Instruct them to do what is good, to be rich in good works, to be generous and willing to share, storing up treasure for themselves as a good foundation for the coming age, so that they may take hold of what is truly life.
>
> —1 TIMOTHY 6:17–19

I want to unpack five truths from this passage:

1. Paul didn't prohibit believers from being rich; rather, he instructs us how to behave if we happen to be rich.

2. He cautions us not to be arrogant with our wealth. In other words, "Don't flaunt it for the world to see. Don't go out of your way to show people that you have four cars, or live in an expensive home, or own a private jet, or wear shoes that cost $1,000." None of these things are sinful in and of themselves, but if we post pictures on social media that flaunt our money and material possessions, or if we do anything that exhibits a spirit of arrogance about our wealth, we're on the wrong track and being poor witnesses.

3. Paul says that we shouldn't set our hope on wealth. Our trust should ultimately be in the God who gives us wealth, not in the wealth itself.

4. We ought to enjoy all the things God has richly provided. If He has given you wealth, enjoy that blessing. Don't let anyone who may be jealous of your wealth stifle your enjoyment.

5. Paul tells us what we should ultimately do with our wealth: be generous. Generosity is the only antidote for greed.

If you have been blessed with wealth, ask yourself these questions on a regular basis:

- Am I helping those who are less fortunate, whether a homeless stranger, aging parents on a fixed income, or others in need?
- Am I giving to support good causes, such as mission organizations and churches?
- Am I open to the Spirit's leading in how I steward my money and how generous I am with it?

God has given some believers wealth not to hoard but to give away and edify others in the body of Christ. By being generous and sharing with others, believers are storing up treasure for themselves in heaven.

Did you know that Jesus spoke about money more than He spoke about faith and prayer combined? Eleven of His thirty-nine parables involve money, and most contain warnings about being rich. Why is this? Jesus knew that most people are easily corrupted by a love of money. He also knew we have a tendency to misuse it, worship it, trust in it, hoard it, and flaunt it. So stay on guard if you've been blessed with any kind of financial security, and check your heart regularly to ensure that your wealth is not having a corrupting influence on you. Beyond avoiding these pitfalls, focus on being a good steward of the material blessings God has given you.

A HEALTHY BALANCE

How should Christians regard health and wealth?

- Reject the idea that God has promised these things to every believer in this life. Scripture is clear that believers are not exempt from suffering and that we should even expect to suffer as we follow the way of Jesus (1 Peter 4:1, 12–13).
- If you are in good health, thank God for this gift every day, because many suffer with poor health and will not be healed this side of heaven.
- While some will not find healing on this earth, when people we know and love are ill, ask God to be gracious and heal them.
- Reject the idea that poverty glorifies God any more than prosperity does.
- Apply biblical principles to save money, get out of debt, invest, and steward your finances wisely.

- Be generous stewards with the wealth God has given, without flaunting it.
- Be vigilant about helping as many people as possible escape the false and dangerous teachings of the prosperity gospel.

THREE

DO I REALLY HAVE THE POWER TO SPEAK THINGS INTO EXISTENCE?

J arren's quest to find the right church continued. At this point he would simply settle for friends he could have genuine, authentic community with—and that's exactly what he thought he had found. Some young people in his apartment complex had started an in-home Bible study on Sunday nights. To Jarren, this was the perfect solution. He knew he needed spiritual community, but the whole local church thing had left him extremely jaded. No surprise, considering what he had experienced thus far! So when he was invited to attend a Sunday-night Bible study, he was elated.

With each session Jarren felt more comfortable with the others in the group, and he even mustered the courage to share his testimony and a bit about his frustrating journey to find the right church. The others seemed to understand, which only made Jarren feel more at home with his newfound community.

But in the weeks that followed, Jarren started noticing tendencies and warning signs that reminded him of his past church experiences. Only now the focus on health and wealth wasn't so overt.

One Sunday morning Jarren woke up feeling like he might be getting a slight cold, but he wasn't going to miss that evening's Bible study for anything—it was his weekly lifeline. At the beginning of the study, everyone took turns expressing how they were doing. When it was Jarren's turn, he shared, "I think I might be getting a cold."

"Jarren, don't say that!" one of the leaders exclaimed.

"Why not?" Jarren asked.

"Because there's power in your words. Don't speak sickness over yourself. When you speak something, the Bible says you can actually speak things into existence."

"Really?" Jarren's jaw dropped.

"Yeah, the Bible says, 'Death and life are in the power of the tongue.'"

Jarren's skepticism must have been written all over his face, because the leader continued, "When you want to experience something in your life, begin speaking it. Begin with affirmations that are consistent with what you want to obtain. If you emit positive energy and have positive thoughts, it's only a matter of time before you'll attract those things into your life."

While Jarren's guard was still up, he'd come to love and trust these people, so he asked, "Has this actually worked for you?"

One girl nodded vigorously. "Absolutely! About this time last year, I manifested my fiancé. I decided I was ready for marriage and began declaring that I would be engaged within a year. And God blessed me to find my soulmate."

Another guy chimed in. "Yep, it worked for me too. I was discontented at my job at my old company, but I started speaking a new start into existence. I manifested it over time, continued to work hard and declare it, and now I am in the career of my dreams."

One by one, everyone shared stories of how they were able to successfully speak things into existence, decreeing and declaring certain blessings over their lives. All of these were blessings Jarren desperately wanted to experience, but he still had questions, especially after his previous church issues. "This sounds a lot like the prosperity gospel, if you ask me."

The leader shook his head. "No, we don't believe in that. What we *do* believe is what we call 'affirmations.' We take what the Word of God says and simply speak it over our lives. Let me give you a few examples."

He reached for his Bible and opened to several bookmarked passages. "In Deuteronomy 28 it says that we are the head and not the tail. So we declare that over our lives. And in the first chapter of Genesis it says that we are to 'be fruitful and multiply,' so those of us who are single are declaring that promise over our lives, believing we will be married. John 8:36 says that Jesus has set us free, so we declare freedom from every addiction over our lives. And in Deuteronomy 8 it says that God has given us the power to get wealth, so we declare that we're financially prosperous in Jesus' name. Does that make sense?"

These positive affirmations seemed backed up with clear, easy-to-understand scriptures. *I might as well give it a shot.* Someone gave Jarren a list of affirmations to recite. Over the next few months he read biblical affirmations related to his job, finances, health, and even a future spouse. He truly hoped and believed that by speaking these over his life, he would see the promises of God fulfilled. But sadly, after months and months of reciting them, nothing in his life had changed.

Finally Jarren took a risk during a conversation with one of his friends. After expressing his frustration with the ineffective affirmations, he was surprised to hear that his friend shared the same frustration. Like Jarren, they had been reciting affirmations over their life but still hadn't seen results.

Then his friend made a comment that helped everything click into place: "You know, I wonder if the problem with these affirmations is that they are man-centered and taken out of context. Just because they are using Scripture doesn't mean they are interpreting it correctly. Affirmations are cool as long as they are God-centered and rooted in biblical truth. But I'm realizing that the affirmations they've been giving us are neither. Maybe that's why they aren't working."

Jarren left that conversation both elated and frustrated. He was elated because he had embraced the truth that you can't simply speak your hopes and dreams into existence. But he felt frustrated because he had wasted more time trying to find a spiritual community he could bond with, only to be disappointed and disillusioned again.

THE POWER OF WORDS

In some Christian circles it's common to hear people speak about the power of words. You might hear someone say, "Don't speak that over your life," or "I speak healing over this situation," or "Ooh, don't say that. You don't want to speak negative things into existence," or "I decree and declare" something or other.

While these Christians probably mean well, behind their statements is the false belief that words have power to create or manifest something. Yes, our words have power, and we *should* be careful how we use them. But does the Bible really say that we can speak things into existence? What does it teach us about the power of our words?

In the previous chapter we spoke about a collection of teachings called the prosperity gospel. One of the primary groups that promote prosperity theology is the Word of Faith movement, and within this movement is a practice called *positive confession*. While the Word of Faith movement is in many ways synonymous with the health-and-wealth false gospel, in this chapter I want to focus on a particular nuance of this view.

First we'll discuss what positive confession is (as well as the closely related idea that we are all "little gods") and explore its origins. We'll also discuss why this false teaching is so dangerous to believers and whether Christians can actually manifest things. Finally, we'll examine what the Bible really says about the power of words in a believer's life.

WHAT IS POSITIVE CONFESSION?

Positive confession is the idea that certain blessings are available to believers at will. We pull down these blessings by positively confessing that they belong to us already. To put it another way, "Positive confession is the practice of saying aloud what you want to happen with the expectation that God will make it a reality."[1]

This practice can be summarized with the short statement, "What I confess, I possess." Hundreds of thousands of Christians have embraced the belief that their words have power to create the reality they desire. This may include a better job, a spouse, health, wealth, or just a better quality of life.

> Positive confession: certain blessings are available to believers at will.

Conversely, this false teaching has caused many to fear speaking the truth about something because they believe their words have power to make it come to pass. For instance, if a person feels a slight cold coming on, they may fear saying, "I feel sick." By confessing that they feel sick, they may actually be inviting the spirit of sickness into their body. I've even heard stories of Christian couples removing the words *in sickness* from their wedding vows because they didn't want to speak sickness into their marriages.

Others are afraid to say, "I'm just so broke I can't afford to do anything." The truth is that they may *not* be able to afford to do what they want to do. But by stating this fact aloud, they fear they're inviting a spirit of poverty into their lives. They're convinced that they shouldn't even speak of financial struggles because they may actually speak poverty into existence.

ORIGINS OF THE POSITIVE CONFESSION MOVEMENT

The Bible says, "What has been is what will be, and what has been done is what will be done; there is nothing new under the sun" (Ecclesiastes 1:9). In other words, many things that people claim are new are actually just something old that is being recycled. This is the case with positive confession and the entire Word of Faith movement.

Scholars debate the exact origins of Word of Faith theology, but it bears a striking resemblance to a secular teaching called New Thought, whose origins date back to the nineteenth century. Although most contemporary Christians have never heard of the New Thought movement, the prosperity gospel has repackaged those ideas with new faces, new technology, new venues, and a slightly altered message.[2]

Some of the leading voices of the New Thought movement included Emanuel Swedenborg, Phineas Quimby, Ralph Waldo Trine, and Norman Vincent Peale. To illustrate the striking similarity between this movement and positive confession theology, consider a few quotes from founders and leading voices of the nineteenth-century movement.

According to Phineas Parkhurst Quimby, "If I believe I am sick, I am sick, for my feelings are my sickness, and my sickness is my belief, and my belief is my mind. Therefore all disease is in the mind or belief."[3] Ralph Waldo Trine reframed the notion of a personal God as the "Infinite Power" or "Infinite Spirit," a kind of energy source that can be harnessed through the power of thought:

> He who lives in the realization of his oneness with this Infinite Power becomes a magnet to attract to himself a continual supply of whatsoever things he desires. . . . If one holds himself in the thought of poverty, he will be poor. . . . if he holds himself. . . . continuously in the thought of prosperity, he sets into operation forces that will sooner or later bring him into prosperous conditions.[4]

Further, Trine claimed, "Very clearly, the life of this Infinite Spirit, from its very nature, can admit of no disease; and if this is true, no disease can exist in the body where it freely enters, through which it freely flows."[5] David Jones and Russell Woodbridge provide a helpful interpretation of Trine's words: "If the Infinite Spirit cannot admit disease into the body, then the culprit must be your mind; you broke a universal law whether you intended to or not."[6]

Continuing with the idea of words containing power, Trine shared this quote from a physician in the movement: "Never affirm or repeat about your health what you do not wish to be true. Do not dwell upon your ailments, nor study your symptoms. Never allow yourself to be convinced that you are not complete master of yourself. Stoutly affirm your superiority over bodily ills, and do not acknowledge yourself the slave of any inferior power."[7]

Wow! This sounds pretty much like what we hear today, doesn't it? As New Thought views developed in the secular world, certain Christian preachers started incorporating them into the church. Let's examine how these principles fused with Christian ideas to form an especially misleading—and alluring—false teaching.

WHY IS WORD OF FAITH THEOLOGY SO ATTRACTIVE?

To uncover the fallacy behind this teaching and show how false teachers twist the Bible to lure well-meaning Christians into believing it, let's consider an example from Genesis 1:26–27: "God said, 'Let us make man in our image, according to our likeness. They will rule the fish of the sea, the birds of the sky, the livestock, the whole earth, and the creatures that crawl on the earth.' So God created man in his own image; he created him in the image of God; he created them male and female."

From this foundational verse, many have reached three false conclusions:

1. Since we have been created in God's image, we have the same power and authority God possesses.
2. Because God used His words to create the universe out of nothing, we can do the same since we were created in His image.
3. God has given us dominion over this world.

All three are faulty conclusions. The Bible never suggests that since we're created in God's image, we somehow have the same power and authority God possesses. Without going too far into the theological weeds, Christian theologians have called some of God's attributes *communicable* and others *noncommunicable.* Communicable attributes are qualities and characteristics God shares with us, since we are indeed created in His image. God is loving, and therefore we have the capacity to love. God is good, and therefore we can be good. God is patient, and therefore we can be patient. God is just, and therefore we can and should be just toward others. Keep in mind that we don't possess or display any of these qualities to the same degree God does. But we are able to share or participate in those qualities by His grace.

Examples of noncommunicable attributes include that God is eternal, having no beginning or end. We aren't eternal in that sense. God is sovereign. We are not. God is all-powerful. We are not. God is all-knowing. We are not. God's creative power is universally understood in historic Christian teaching as a noncommunicable attribute, because He is the Creator and we are creatures. We can reflect God's creativity by putting together preexisting stuff in new ways. We can create art out of paint and canvas or build musical instruments out of wood and metal. But only God has the power to create something out of nothing. So we can immediately shut down the false conclusion from Genesis 1 that we possess God's creative power.

The Bible also doesn't teach that because we're created in God's image, we can simply speak things into existence the way God did when He spoke the words that formed the universe out of nothing. Some will say we have the power to "call those things that are not as though they are." If I were given a dollar every time I heard a Christian use that phrase, I'd be a rich man!

> Only God has the power to create something out of nothing.

What I'm about to share underscores the danger of quoting popular Christian clichés and the importance of knowing the Word of God and understanding how to correctly interpret it. That phrase "call those things that are not as though they are" comes from Romans 4:17, which says, "God . . . gives life to the dead and calls those things which do not exist as though they did" (NKJV).

Let's study the context of this passage (which is always a good idea). The chapter is talking about God's promise to make Abraham the father of many nations, even though his wife, Sarah, was barren. Years went by after Abraham received the promise of a son, and the event still hadn't come to pass. Regardless of what his circumstances were telling him, Abraham believed that God would fulfill His promise. Abraham's faith rested in the fact that God was able to "give life to the dead" and "call those things which do not exist as though they did." This clearly referred to Sarah's barren womb. He believed that God could overcome not only that Abraham was getting old but also that his wife had never given birth and was now well past childbearing years.

Even a cursory reading of this verse shows that *God* alone can speak things into existence. There's no mention of Christians sharing this divine ability. To suggest otherwise is not just a misinterpretation of this verse but also an obvious misreading of it.

THE LITTLE GODS DOCTRINE

The idea of positive confession within the Word of Faith movement rests on a deeper, more involved, and dangerous false teaching called the little gods doctrine. I don't use the word *heresy* lightly, but it clearly applies here. Many of the most popular Word of Faith teachers are promoting this heresy and leading many astray. Instead of summarizing this false teaching, I want you to hear it straight from the pastors and teachers who promote it.

In a sermon, televangelist Creflo Dollar promoted the foundational idea of the little gods doctrine: we are the same *kind* of being as God Himself.

DOLLAR: "If horses get together, they produce what?"
CONGREGATION: "Horses!"
DOLLAR: "If dogs get together, they produce what?"
CONGREGATION: "Dogs!"
DOLLAR: "If cats get together, they produce what?"
CONGREGATION: "Cats!"
DOLLAR: "So if the Godhead says, 'Let us make *man* in *our* image,' and everything produces after its own kind, then they produce what?"
CONGREGATION: "Gods!"
DOLLAR: "Gods. Little-*g* gods. You're not human. The only human part of you is this flesh you're wearing."[8]

Dollar not only claims divine status for humans but his words also reveal a problematic understanding of what it means to be human. Rather than recognizing that humans are both physical and spiritual, body and soul, he claims that we are gods who are only wearing human bodies.

According to Earl Paulk, "Adam and Eve were placed in the world as the seed and expression of God. Just as dogs have puppies and cats have kittens, so God has little gods. . . . He created us as little gods, but we have trouble comprehending this truth. . . . Until we comprehend that we are little gods . . . , we cannot manifest the Kingdom of God."[9] Popular Word of Faith teacher Kenneth Copeland stated this teaching even more bluntly: "You don't have a God in you; you are one."[10]

Joyce Meyer adds her voice to the chorus, paraphrasing another of the movement's teachers to support her belief:

Why do people have such a fit about God calling His creation, . . . His man . . . "little gods"? If He's God, what's He going to call them but the god-kind? I mean, if you as a human being have a baby, you call it a humankind. If cattle have another cattle, they call it cattle-kind. So, I mean, what's God supposed to call us? Doesn't the Bible say we're created in His image? Now, you understand I am not saying you are God with a capital G.[11]

The distinction Meyer, Dollar, and other Word of Faith teachers make between "God with a capital G" and humans as little gods may seem like a helpful nuance, but it doesn't solve the fundamental problem with the little gods doctrine. Scripture and Christian tradition are united in affirming that there is only *one* God in the proper sense. Historic, traditional Christianity has long held that God is not just the best or most powerful member of a species; he is the *only* God.

Kenneth Hagin, considered by many to be the founder of the Word of Faith movement, claimed, "You are as much the incarnation of God as Jesus Christ was. Every man who has been born again is an incarnation and Christianity is a miracle. The believer is as much an incarnation as was Jesus of Nazareth."[12] To suggest that anyone other than Jesus was God incarnate is blasphemy and heresy. This teaching seems to suggest that the delineation between Jesus and those He came to save should be minimized.

Other notable Word of Faith teachers, such as Benny Hinn, Paula White, T. D. Jakes, and Joel Osteen, have also affirmed their belief in the little gods doctrine. Every false doctrine is based on a misinterpretation of particular verses in Scripture. One of the key verses for the little gods doctrine is Psalm 82:6: "You are gods; you are all sons of the Most High." Based on this verse and others like it, those who promote the little gods doctrine claim that we are the same *kind* of being as God and that certain powers or abilities come along with this identity—namely, that we possess the power of the Most High God. Let's apply two of the most basic interpretational principles to see if this claim holds true. First, let's look at the *context*, starting with the beginning of Psalm 82: "God stands in the divine assembly; he pronounces judgment among the gods: 'How long will you judge unjustly and show partiality to the wicked?'" (verses 1–2).

The psalmist envisioned God pronouncing judgment in the assembly of these wicked judges who were called gods, not because they have the same creative power as God but because they are God's representatives to the people. They were supposed to exercise the authority God gave them to judge properly, but they were judging unjustly, showing partiality to the wicked in court. The psalm continues: "Provide justice for the needy and the fatherless; uphold the rights of the oppressed and the destitute. Rescue the poor and needy; save them from the power of the wicked" (Psalm 82:3–4).

Here the psalmist was pleading with these unjust judges to provide justice for the needy and the fatherless, who were being oppressed by wicked people. As God's representatives, the judges were to execute justice. "They do not know or understand; they wander in darkness.

All the foundations of the earth are shaken. I said, 'You are gods; you are all sons of the Most High'" (Psalm 82:5–6).

Although many Word of Faith proponents use this passage to suggest that we are little gods, the word *gods* here clearly refers to a position of authority. According to one commentary, "The crucial question of interpretation involves the meaning of gods (*elohîm*) in verses 1 and 6. These may be . . . human judges ('mighty ones') who are 'gods' because they exercise divine justice, having received the word of God. Thus they are not gods by nature but have a godlike function in bringing justice to the world and in judging human life."[13]

In other words, God has appointed men to positions of authority in which they are considered gods among the people. But even though they are representing God in this world, they are mortal and must eventually give an account to Him for how they used that authority.

The next verses make it abundantly clear that whatever being called "little gods" involves, it doesn't actually include divine status or the kind of power and authority that go along with that. "'However, you will die like humans and fall like any other ruler.' Rise up, God, judge the earth, for all the nations belong to you" (Psalm 82:7–8).

The context here does not allow for us to conclude that we are little gods in the sense that many Word of Faith teachers claim.

> Being called "little gods" doesn't include divine status or its power and authority.

This is a classic example of why context is so critical for a proper understanding of the Bible. I hope you're seeing a pattern here. Many of the false teachings that are being promoted in our churches today are derived from a faulty interpretation of the Bible in which basic interpretational and exegetical principles are neglected.

Now let's move on to the second interpretational principle: *cross-references*, which are passages with similar phrases, concepts, or themes. The goal is to use clear, easy-to-understand passages to help us interpret difficult passages. So we're going to look at what the rest of the Bible says about the existence of other gods besides the one true God.

> "You are my witnesses"—this is the LORD's declaration—"and my servant whom I have chosen, so that you may know and believe me and understand that I am he. No god was formed before me, and there will be none after me."
>
> —ISAIAH 43:10

> This is what the LORD, the King of Israel and its Redeemer, the LORD of Armies, says: I am the first and I am the last. There is no God but me.
>
> —ISAIAH 44:6

> Even if there are so-called gods, whether in heaven or on earth—as there are many "gods" and many "lords"—yet for us there is one God, the Father. All things are from him, and we exist for him. And there is one Lord, Jesus Christ. All things are through him, and we exist through him.
>
> —1 CORINTHIANS 8:5–6

The Bible cannot contradict itself. Again and again, God makes the claim that there are no other gods but Him. To assert otherwise is heresy. We can conclude based on the principles of context and cross-referencing that any doctrine that says we are little gods in the sense that we are the same kind of being as God Himself, sharing in His unique attributes, power, or authority, must be a false doctrine.

PROBLEMS WITH POSITIVE CONFESSION

Now that we have dispelled the idea that we are little gods, let's return to the matter at hand. What exactly is the problem with positive confession? I mean, at the end of the day, what is so wrong with speaking the Word of God over your life?

Problem #1: A Misunderstanding of Scripture

Many of the scriptures that positive confession proponents use as promises from God are taken out of context and therefore misunderstood. Here's one example: "Dear friend, I pray that you are prospering in every way and are in good health, just as your whole life is going well" (3 John 2).

Instead of simply interpreting this verse as saying, "Hey, man, I hope and pray all is well in your life and that you're getting along well," some Word of Faith proponents turn this scripture into a promise from God for prosperity and good health. But John was simply greeting the recipient of this letter and expressing his desire for that person's well-being. It was a comment directed to a specific person in a particular situation, not a general principle that applies to all believers.

Another example is Deuteronomy 8:18, which says, "Remember that the LORD your God gives you the power to gain wealth, in order to confirm his covenant he swore to your ancestors, as it is today."

Some Word of Faith proponents take this to mean that we should claim the power to gain wealth that God has given us. God can give anyone the power to gain wealth, and He may well give particular believers today the wisdom and ability to make money and manage it effectively. But this is not a promise from God! Moses was merely reminding the Israelites not to forget God when they entered the promised land. God gave them the power to obtain this wealthy land on His way to fulfilling His specific promises to *them*. This is not a promise to us today.

You can probably see a common theme here in how Word of Faith teachers misuse Scripture. In short, "People who push positive confession say that the practice is merely restating God's promises as given in the Bible. But they don't differentiate between universal promises God made to all His followers (e.g., Philippians 4:19) and personal promises made to individuals at a certain time for a particular purpose (e.g., Jeremiah 29:11)."[14]

There are many more examples of misinterpreting Scripture and the promises of God, but I want you to see one thing clearly. Many positive confession teachers use Scripture in just about everything that they teach, but it's essential to discern whether it's being used *properly*. Study the verse or passage for yourself and make sure that the teacher isn't twisting it to say something it's not.

Problem #2: A Misunderstanding of Faith

Another way the positive confession movement misleads or deceives many well-meaning Christians is by teaching incorrect things about faith.

The roots of the Word of Faith movement and the name it and claim it message have more in common with new age metaphysics than with biblical Christianity. However, instead of us creating our reality with our thoughts, as new age proponents advise, name it and claim it teachers tell us that we can use the "power of faith" to create our own reality or get what we want. In essence, *faith* is redefined from "a trust in a holy and sovereign God" to "a way of controlling God to give us what we want." Faith becomes a force whereby we can get what we want rather than an abiding trust in God even during times of trials and suffering.[15]

Our faith should be in a person—the Lord Jesus Christ—not in faith itself. In other words, we shouldn't have faith in our faith. Faith should also not be used to manipulate God to give us what we want.

Problem #3: A Misunderstanding of Reality

Positive confession proponents have a difficult time accepting the reality that not only is life tough but the Bible promises that we will experience suffering and hardship (as we discussed in the chapter on health and wealth). We can and should acknowledge these realities without fearing that we will negate our blessings. Let's take a moment to clear up the confusion about negative confession.

As we discussed earlier, the positive confession movement has caused many Christians to live in fear of acknowledging any sort of reality because it might attract negative things into their lives or some-how negate what God has promised them. But verbally acknowledging our pain, depression, poverty, and sickness is not only healthy but also biblical. Throughout the Psalms, David acknowledged his pain to God: "Why, my soul, are you so dejected? Why are you in such turmoil? Put your hope in God, for I will still praise him, my Savior and my God. . . . I will say to God, my rock, 'Why have you forgotten me? Why must I go about in sorrow because of the enemy's oppression?'" (Psalm 42:5, 9).

These verses give us a sneak peek into the heart posture of David. And lest there be any uncertainty about whether we should follow his example, consider his words of encouragement: "Cast your burden on the LORD, and he will sustain you; he will never allow the righteous to be shaken" (Psalm 55:22). Throughout the Scriptures we are encouraged to express and acknowledge the reality of our pain to God and to others. And nowhere in the Bible does it suggest that speaking about our negative reality causes God to withhold certain blessings from us.

Another reality that positive confession proponents don't acknowledge is that positive confession just doesn't work! I'm not sure how much more bluntly I can put it. All you have to do is try to speak into existence becoming debt-free in a year. Simply speaking the words isn't going to create the reality. Certainly there are examples where God has blessed a person with a financial increase that wiped all of their debt away, but those kinds of miraculous interventions are few and far between. The norm is that people must apply biblical principles for saving and getting out of debt rather than trusting God for a quick fix to their financial struggles.

Or try speaking a child into existence by next year if you've been unable to conceive due to medical complications. If indeed we are little gods who possess creative power as God does, we should be able to speak things into existence with our words the way He did at the beginning of time. But the reality is that we are not little gods, and God Himself has limited the power our words possess.

WHAT ABOUT MANIFESTATION?

I'd be remiss if I didn't address a more recent trend sweeping across our world today: the idea of *manifestation*. This buzzword is becoming increasingly popular even among Christians. Maybe you've heard a fellow believer say, "I manifested my new house," or "I manifested my soulmate," or "I manifested my business success."

Although this is closely connected to the idea of speaking things into existence, it focuses a bit more on a person's mindset rather than just the words they speak. Proponents of manifestation believe that if you *think* positively enough about something, you can manifest it into existence. If you believe something in your heart hard enough, it will come true.

Like Word of Faith theology, the idea of manifestation emerged from New Thought ideology, specifically the so-called law of attraction.

Though manifestation ideology has its roots in the writings of New Thought leaders like Phineas Quimby and Prentice Mulford in the 1800s, the New Age movement picked it up and popularized it for general audiences in books like *The Secret*, published in 2006. Those who practice manifestation believe that "whatever vibe you think or 'put out' will come back to you. If you think good thoughts, good will come back to you; however, if you think negative thoughts, negative things will happen in your life."[16]

As warm and fuzzy as this may sound, as believers we must always measure what we do, think, and believe against Scripture. There are several problems associated with this concept of manifesting.

First, it steals the glory from God and places it on the person doing the manifesting. Scripture tells us that "every good and perfect gift is from above, coming down from the Father of lights, who does not change like shifting shadows" (James 1:17). This verse makes it abundantly clear that any good gift we receive is from God and not from ourselves.

While there is a place for hard work, determination, and discipline, as Christians we ultimately recognize God as the source of all our blessings. Manifesting essentially turns each of us into our own god. No longer do we need to have faith in God's all-sufficient ability to provide for our needs. Rather, we can trust in our own ability to attract good things to ourselves. This explicitly contradicts Scripture:

Trust in the LORD with all your heart, and do not rely on your own understanding; in all your ways know him, and he will make your paths straight.

—PROVERBS 3:5–6

A person's heart plans his way, but the LORD determines his steps.

—PROVERBS 16:9

Many plans are in a person's heart, but the Lord's decree will prevail.

—Proverbs 19:21

Another problem with manifesting is that we assume *we* know what's best for us without consulting the God who knows all. Furthermore, while something may be right for us, the timing we have in mind may not be right. When we attempt to manifest something, we don't consider God's will or His timing. We consider only our own desires.

Finally, manifestation often uses concepts like meditation and mantras to bring about a desired result. While the Bible clearly encourages us to meditate, the *object* of our meditation is critical. Meditating on Scripture and God's sovereignty is a practice believers should engage in. Meditating to bring about a desired result is unbiblical and simply a waste of time. Additionally, while the Bible does encourage us to think positively (Philippians 4:8) and to have a vision for our lives, we as finite beings must always submit our thoughts, desires, goals, dreams, and visions to a sovereign God who knows the type and timing of every blessing.

A BIBLICAL APPROACH TO THE POWER OF WORDS

Now that we've debunked the idea of positive confession, let's explore the power our words do have. The Bible says, "Death and life are in the power of the tongue, and those who love it will eat its fruit" (Proverbs 18:21). What exactly does this mean?

Clearly there's some sense in which our words have the power of life and death. My goal is to encourage you to focus on using your words in ways that align with the Bible and not in the unbiblical ways many Word of Faith teachers promote. How do our words create life? Let's go directly to Scripture.

Our Words Can Build Others Up

Scripture tells us that God has given us the ability to use our words to encourage and edify others:

> No foul language should come from your mouth, but only what is good for building up someone in need, so that it gives grace to those who hear.
>
> —EPHESIANS 4:29

> Encourage each other daily, while it is still called today, so that none of you is hardened by sin's deception.
>
> —HEBREWS 3:13

> Not neglecting to gather together, as some are in the habit of doing, but encouraging each other, and all the more as you see the day approaching.
>
> —HEBREWS 10:25

When people around us are experiencing discouragement, we have the power to infuse courage into their hearts.

Our Words Can Intercede for Others

The Bible also instructs us to pray for others: "Therefore, confess your sins to one another and pray for one another, so that you may be healed. The prayer of a righteous person is very powerful in its effect" (James 5:16).

I would encourage you not just to pray *for* others but to pray *with* others. There is power in hearing someone else pray God's will and His promises over your life. Our prayers are so powerful that, according to this verse, God may respond to our intercession and faith for those who are sick and actually heal them! Note, however, that the decision to heal is totally up to God and is not contingent upon how much faith we muster during the prayer.

Our Words Can Advise Others

The Bible says, "Listen to counsel and receive instruction so that you may be wise later in life" (Proverbs 19:20). When people have difficult decisions to make, God's Spirit can lead us to give sound biblical wisdom. Your words could ultimately change the trajectory of someone's life for the better.

Our Words Can Heal Others

"There is one who speaks rashly, like a piercing sword; but the tongue of the wise brings healing" (Proverbs 12:18). This verse isn't talking about physical healing but about the ability to promote emotional healing within an individual. When we are Spirit-led, God can use us to speak life into someone's soul, bringing spiritual healing.

> God can use us to speak life into someone's soul, bringing spiritual healing.

While we're on this topic, I want to caution you *not* to use your words negatively. When we constantly criticize people and point out their flaws, we create *death* with our words. Our words can lead to the death of a person's self-confidence, causing them to buy into the lie that they will never measure up. Our words of criticism can result in the death of someone's dream. And words of gossip and slander can result in the death of a person's reputation. So make it your goal to speak words of life and healing into those around you.

A HEALTHY BALANCE

Our words have power, but not the type of power that many Word of Faith proponents claim. God doesn't submit to our words. We cannot create things with our words. We cannot speak things into existence. We cannot "call those things that are not as though they are." Christians shouldn't live in fear that speaking about the negative realities of life will give power to them and attract negative results.

If we're sick, we should acknowledge that we're sick without fear that our words may promote or prolong our sickness. Instead, we should bridle our tongues and be careful to use our words wisely as we engage with others. Finally, we should avoid any belief or teaching that suggests we can create our own destinies, whether through our words or our thoughts. Such beliefs diverge from biblical Christianity and delve into New Thought and New Age practices that are contrary to God's ways.

FOUR

WHAT ABOUT PROPHETS AND PROPHECY?

Despite his intense frustration after wasting months as part of the positive-affirmation community, Jarren knew fellowship with other believers brought him closer to God. He kept trying to find the right church. Many of his friends attended a place called House of Prophecy, so he decided to give it a try. After Jarren had attended for a few weeks, one of his friends, Matthew, asked, "Got any plans for Friday night?"

"Not right now," Jarren replied. "Why? What's up?"

"You should really consider attending this special prophetic service. One of the most popular and anointed prophets will be in town, and he'll speak prophecies over people's lives."

At this point, considering his most recent experiences with church, Jarren was a bit skeptical. "Hmm. I think I'll pass. But let me know how it goes."

"Are you sure?" Matthew obviously wasn't ready to let this go. "I really believe that God told me to invite you to come. He spoke to me in a dream last night about you."

If God has really spoken to Matthew, who am I to keep pushing back? Jarren studied his friend's earnest expression and shrugged his shoulders. "Okay, okay. I'll come."

"Good!" Matthew slapped him on the shoulder. "I'll see you on Friday night. Let's meet in the foyer so we can get good seats. The anointing of God seems to fall more in the front than in the back."

By Friday night Jarren was starting to feel excited. He'd never attended a prophetic service before. He met Matthew in the foyer, they found their seats, and Jarren was quickly immersed in the worship experience. After being out of church for some time, his heart was tender and he felt ready to receive whatever word God had for him that night.

As the worship time concluded, a man came onto the stage imploring people to give money to the church. He quoted a scripture about the importance of sowing and reaping a tenfold blessing. Considering the churches Jarren had previously attended, his defenses immediately went up. *No way am I going to give.* This went on for about thirty minutes, and Jarren began getting restless. *When are we gonna get to the prophetic stuff?* he wondered.

Finally, ninety minutes into the service, a broad-shouldered man in a suit walked onstage and began prophesying. His posture shouted of confidence and power as he scanned the sanctuary. "There is someone here who had a fight with their spouse just this morning. God wants you to come down right now."

A middle-aged woman approached the stage, and the prophet continued, "Today God wants you to know that your struggles in your marriage are over. I declare it and decree it in the name of Jesus." The woman walked away celebrating, appearing confident that her marriage would immediately improve.

The prophet studied the crowd for a moment before continuing. "There is someone here who has recently been diagnosed with stage-four cancer. God wants you to know today that you are healed in the name of Jesus!"

Another man jumped out of his seat and began to shout for joy. Jarren thought, *Wow, how does this man know these things? I hope I can get a prophetic word!*

The service continued at a rapid pace, with the prophet speaking messages and people scattered throughout the sanctuary reacting to his words with shock, joy, and—always—complete belief that it was truth. "There is someone here who recently lost a loved one, very close to them, to cancer. God wants you to know today that He's going to restore you. He's going to bless you. In ninety days God's going to replace that which has been taken from you and bless you tenfold. The person God will bring into your life will soften the pain of the person you just lost. Receive that word right now in the name of Jesus."

Jarren's eyebrows went up and he watched to see if anyone else reacted to this message. *Is this prophetic word meant for me?* It felt like exactly what he needed to hear after recently losing Sarah. Was God speaking to him through the prophet? He walked out of the service excited and hopeful that God would bring a tenfold blessing into his life—along with someone special who would help him work through the pain of his loss.

But Jarren also had questions. *Was I the only one there who lost someone to cancer? What exactly does a tenfold blessing look like? Who exactly is this person God wants to bring into my life?*

Seeking out his friends who attended the church, Jarren shared his hopes and confusions, but they urged him not to question the prophet. "You should simply receive the word from God!"

Ninety days passed and nothing significant changed in Jarren's life. No tenfold blessing. No new person to ease the grief of losing Sarah. Because of his earlier church experience, Jarren had decided not to get his hopes up about receiving a financial blessing. But he still had hopes of receiving other parts of a prophetic word. And yet the days of waiting turned into weeks and then months—and still no one special came into his life. *Why would God get my hopes up that something special would happen? What kind of God makes promises and doesn't fulfill them?*

Jarren eventually left that church as well, only this time he was questioning not only God but also his faith. Perplexed and disillusioned, he started to drift spiritually. He was beginning to think that God didn't care about him at all.

THE HARM CAUSED BY FALSE PROPHETS

Jarren's experience is far too common and highlights the extreme danger of regarding a self-proclaimed prophet's words as authoritative or divine revelation from God.

A prophetic experience typically looks something like this: A self-proclaimed prophet speaks a prophetic word over someone's life or over different people in a group setting. Those to whom the word applies assume it's from God based on the authority the prophet claims and the charisma with which the word is delivered. They get their hopes up, believing that God has something special in store for them. Then they wait expectantly. But when enough time passes and they finally realize nothing is happening, they start to get angry—not at the prophet but at God. They conclude that God must have failed them.

Because so many have been misled by an incorrect or incomplete understanding of prophecy, this chapter will focus on clearing up the confusion and providing a balanced and biblical view of this spiritual gift.

WHAT IS THE GIFT OF PROPHECY?

To evaluate the validity of modern-day prophecy, it's critical for us to first explore the role and function of a prophet in the Bible. Many people assume that a prophet is simply someone who can predict the future. However, as I will demonstrate, the primary role of a biblical prophet was so much more than that. As we explore what the Bible says about a prophet's primary functions, I invite you to think about whether they are reflected in people who claim to be prophets today.

Prophecy in the Old Testament

In the Old Testament, God instituted different offices among the people of Israel. One of these offices was that of priest. A priest spoke to God on behalf of the people, among other duties. But another office, the office of prophet, involved speaking to the people on behalf of God, and prophetic messages usually had one or more of the following purposes.

Prophets Exposed Sinful Practices

One of the prophet's primary functions was to expose the sinful practices of the people, especially their idolatry, the practice of worshiping other gods. The prophet Micah spoke these words to the people of Israel: "I will remove your carved images and sacred pillars from you so that you will no longer worship the work of your hands" (Micah 5:13).

Speaking through the prophet Jeremiah, God Himself called out the people's idolatry: "I will pronounce my judgments against them for all the evil they did when they abandoned me to burn incense to other gods and to worship the works of their own hands" (Jeremiah 1:16).

Habakkuk echoed a similar warning: "Woe to him who says to wood: Wake up! or to mute stone: Come alive! Can it teach? Look! It may be plated with gold and silver, yet there is no breath in it at all" (Habakkuk 2:19).

The people of Israel frequently fell into the sin of worshiping other gods in place of the one true God. The prophets were quick to call them out on it. The prophets also called out the horrible sin of child sacrifice. To put this in context, some of the pagan nations surrounding Israel sacrificed their children to idols. Israel began to adopt this practice, and God called on the prophets to warn the people: "When you offer your gifts, sacrificing your children in the fire, you still continue to defile yourselves with all your idols today. So should I let you inquire of me, house of Israel? As I live—this is the declaration of the Lord GOD—I will not let you inquire of me!" (Ezekiel 20:31).

Jeremiah rebuked the people for the same sin: "They have built the high places of Baal in Ben Hinnom Valley to sacrifice their sons and daughters in the fire to Molech—something I had not commanded them. I had never entertained the thought that they do this detestable act causing Judah to sin!" (Jeremiah 32:35).

God also commissioned prophets to call out the sins of injustice and oppression of the poor. For example, the prophet Isaiah was highly focused on injustices among God's people:

> Learn to do what is good. Pursue justice. Correct the oppressor. Defend the rights of the fatherless. Plead the widow's cause.
>
> —ISAIAH 1:17

> The LORD brings this charge against the elders and leaders of his people: "You have devastated the vineyard. The plunder from the poor is in your houses. Why do you crush my people and grind the faces of the poor?" This is the declaration of the Lord GOD of Armies.
>
> —ISAIAH 3:14–15

Another sin the prophets called out was sexual immorality. In the book of Amos it says, "They trample the heads of the poor on the dust of the ground and obstruct the path of the needy. A man and his father have sexual relations with the same girl, profaning my holy name" (2:7).

As we assess those who claim to be prophets today, we must ensure that they follow in the footsteps of the Old Testament prophets. A considerable portion of their message should be dedicated to exposing the sinful practices that our society faces—including abortion, sexual sin, and social injustices—and calling people to holiness. While this doesn't need to be the only focus of their message, given the role of the Old Testament prophets, we should see that same emphasis with anyone who claims to be a prophet today.

Prophets Called People to Repentance

After a prophet exposed the sinful practices of the people, the natural next step was to call them to repentance. A great example of this is in the book of Joel:

> Even now—this is the LORD's declaration—
> turn to me with all your heart,
> with fasting, weeping, and mourning.
> Tear your hearts,
> not just your clothes,
> and return to the LORD your God.
> For he is gracious and compassionate,
> slow to anger, abounding in faithful love,
> and he relents from sending disaster.
> Who knows? He may turn and relent
> and leave a blessing behind him,
> so you can offer a grain offering and a drink offering
> to the LORD your God.
>
> —JOEL 2:12–14

Hosea issued a similar call to repentance in his prophecy:

> Israel, return to the LORD your God,
> for you have stumbled in your iniquity.
> Take words of repentance with you
> and return to the LORD.
> Say to him, "Forgive all our iniquity

and accept what is good,

so that we may repay you

with praise from our lips."

—Hosea 14:1–2

These prophets genuinely cared about the spiritual condition of their people and didn't want to see God's judgment poured out, so they actively and passionately implored the people to repent. When the people refused, these prophets were so heartbroken that many of them wept, mourned, and fasted. Their main focus was the spiritual condition of the people, not their physical or material condition.

> Modern-day prophets must focus on an individual's spiritual condition.

So once again, as we assess the validity of modern-day prophets, they must focus primarily on an individual's spiritual condition, not just their physical wellness or material possessions.

Prophets Warned People of Impending Danger

After a prophet made the people aware of their sin and called them to repent, their third primary function was to warn of the consequences of continuing to rebel against God. This is where we see a distinct break between the true prophets in the Old Testament and many people who claim to be prophets today.

Old Testament prophets were hated because they delivered messages from God that people didn't want to hear. Let's be honest: Who wants to hear that if they don't repent and turn from their sin, they can expect God's judgment? That's not a popular message. For that reason, the prophets were hated, persecuted, and even killed at the hands of godless people. The role of a prophet wasn't glamorous. They were literally risking their lives. God made this abundantly clear to the prophet Ezekiel:

> Son of man, I have made you a watchman over the house of Israel. When you hear a word from my mouth, give them a warning from me. If I say to the wicked person, "You will surely die," but you do not warn him—you don't speak out to warn him about his wicked way in order to save his life—that wicked person will die for his iniquity. Yet I will hold you responsible for his blood. But if you warn a wicked person and he does not turn from his wickedness or his wicked way, he will die for his iniquity, but you will have rescued yourself.
>
> —EZEKIEL 3:17–19

Wow. That puts things into perspective, doesn't it? These men were under a divine obligation to warn the people of impending judgment. A great example of this is found in the sixth chapter of Amos. To provide some context, Amos prophesied during a time when the nation of Israel was experiencing a degree of peace and prosperity. "Woe to those who are at ease in Zion and to those who feel secure on the hill of Samaria—the notable people in this first of the nations, those the house of Israel comes to" (Amos 6:1).

He continued a few verses later: "The Lord GOD has sworn by himself—this is the declaration of the LORD, the God of Armies: I loathe Jacob's pride and hate his citadels, so I will hand over the city and everything in it. And if there are ten men left in one house, they will die" (Amos 6:8–9). Then he made the warning even more specific: "But look, I am raising up a nation against you, house of Israel—this is the declaration of the Lord, the GOD of Armies—and they will oppress you from the entrance of Hamath to the Brook of the Arabah" (verse 14).

You get the idea. God, through the prophet Amos, was graciously giving these people time to repent by explaining exactly what would happen to them if they didn't.

The prophet Joel also warned God's people of judgment:

> Blow the ram's horn in Zion;
> sound the alarm on my holy mountain!
> Let all the residents of the land tremble,
> for the day of the LORD is coming;
> in fact, it is near—
> a day of darkness and gloom,
> a day of clouds and total darkness,
> like the dawn spreading over the mountains;
> a great and strong people appears,
> such as never existed in ages past
> and never will again
> in all the generations to come.
>
> —JOEL 2:1–2

It's critical at this point to explain the conditional nature of some of these prophecies. Since it was never God's intent or desire to punish His people for their sin, a prophet would often give warnings of judgment, and if the people repented, God would relent from punishing them. The Lord explained this through the prophet Jeremiah: "At one moment I might announce concerning a nation or a kingdom that I will uproot, tear down, and destroy it. However, if that nation about which I have made the announcement turns from its evil, I will relent concerning the disaster I had planned to do to it" (Jeremiah 18:7–8).

We see a similar conditional prophecy in the book of Jonah. Jonah went to Nineveh and announced, "In forty days Nineveh will be demolished!" (Jonah 3:4). This should be seen as a warning, with the intent to give people time to repent. They did repent and the city was spared (Jonah 3:8–10). We should expect any self-proclaimed prophet today to focus a considerable portion of their message on calling people to repentance—including giving biblical examples of what happens when people don't repent and continue in willful sin.

How Were Prophets Regarded?

Another major point of consideration is how the Israelites regarded the Old Testament prophets compared with how people view self-proclaimed prophets today. Prophets today are often revered, respected, and admired. People who would like to be prophets themselves usually covet the center-stage gifts of well-known prophets. Many of these prophets have luxurious lives (nothing is inherently wrong with that, by the way). But the way modern-day prophets are regarded is starkly different from how Old Testament prophets were viewed. Consider the following:

1. Amos was told to go away. "Then Amaziah said to Amos, 'Go away, you seer! Flee to the land of Judah. Earn your living and give your prophecies there'" (Amos 7:12). People rejected rather than welcomed the prophets because they typically didn't prophesy good things.

2. Jeremiah was beaten and imprisoned. "The officials were angry at Jeremiah and beat him and placed him in jail in the house of Jonathan the scribe, for it had been made into a prison" (Jeremiah 37:15). This happened because the people didn't want to hear what Jeremiah was saying.

I'm sharing these examples to show the vast difference between modern-day prophets and the prophets in the Old Testament. When you believe that a prophet is going to prophesy something good over you, of course you welcome them! That is what many modern-day prophets are doing, or expected to do, which is why their services are generally filled with people.

> The prophets seldom promised anything good. They predicted God's judgment.

To summarize, the prophets in the Old Testament seldom promised anything good. Rather, they predicted God's judgment. Their messages convicted the people of sin. They were telling people things they didn't want to hear. For that reason, the prophets were hated, not loved. They were persecuted, not celebrated. People ran away from them rather than toward them.

Prophecy in the New Testament

Now that we understand how prophets functioned in the Old Testament, how should we regard prophecy in the New Testament? Before we examine this, we must first ask and answer the question, "Has the gift of prophecy ceased?" This is heavily debated, and both sides have strong, Bible-believing Christians with different views.

One camp argues that the gift of prophecy ceased when the writing of Scripture was completed at the end of the first century. The idea is that the gift of prophecy was no longer necessary since God has already revealed everything we need to know about His will through the Scriptures. Others believe that the gift of prophecy operates the same today as it always has. Before we proceed further, I want to share my personal position on this important, foundational question so that you know where I'm coming from. Let's walk through the basic arguments for each side.

Those who believe the gift of prophecy has ceased often support their position by referencing 1 Corinthians 13:8–12, which reads,

> Love never ends. But as for prophecies, they will come to an end; as
> for tongues, they will cease; as for knowledge, it will come to an end.
> For we know in part, and we prophesy in part, but when the perfect

comes, the partial will come to an end. When I was a child, I spoke like a child, I thought like a child, I reasoned like a child. When I became a man, I put aside childish things. For now we see only a reflection as in a mirror, but then face to face. Now I know in part, but then I will know fully, as I am fully known.

This verse clearly says "as for prophecies, they will come to an end." No one is arguing that. The point of contention is *when*. When exactly will spiritual gifts (because that is the context of this passage) like tongues, prophecy, and knowledge come to an end? Well, it tells us when. It says, "But when the perfect comes, the partial will come to an end." The question that is heavily debated is, "What or whom does 'the perfect' refer to?"

Those who believe the gift of prophecy has ceased (known as cessationists) support their view by interpreting "the perfect" as the perfect (or completed) New Testament. They assert that when the New Testament canon was closed, God's perfect revelation was sealed, and therefore there is no further need for the prophetic gift. Those who believe the gift of prophecy continues today (continuationists) usually believe that the word *perfect* refers to Jesus and His second coming. So which view is correct? Let's read a little further in 1 Corinthians 13: "For now we see only a reflection as in a mirror, but then face to face. Now I know in part, but then I will know fully, as I am fully known" (verse 12).

Notice that one day we will see "face to face." Concerning this phrase, John Piper wrote,

Is it more likely that Paul is saying, "Now before the New Testament is written, we see in a mirror dimly; but then when the New Testament is written, we shall see face to face"? Or is it more likely that he is saying, "Now in this age we see in a mirror dimly; but then when the

Lord returns, we shall see face to face"? In the Old Testament, there are half a dozen references to seeing God "face to face." Revelation 22:4 says that in heaven we shall see God's face. 1 John 3:2 says that when Jesus appears, we shall be like him for we shall see him as he is.[1]

I concur with Piper here. Continuing on in the passage, Paul said that when the perfect comes, we will "know fully." Once again, Piper provides some insight here: "Now is this a contrast between before and after the New Testament or before and after the second coming? It's hard for me to imagine Paul or any of us saying that after the New Testament was written, we now in this age understand fully, even as we have been fully understood."[2]

It is my personal position (although I deeply respect those who see it differently) that there is not enough biblical evidence to say definitively that the spiritual gift of prophecy has ceased and is no longer active today. For me, the real questions are, "How do you define prophecy?" and "How is this gift being exercised in the New Testament context?"

The Gift of Prophecy in the New Testament

Arriving at an exact definition or description of a prophet in the New Testament proves to be much more difficult compared with the Old Testament. One question that scholars debate is whether prophecy is limited to providing *new* revelation or could include the explanation of *existing* revelation. Those who believe the latter say that forthtelling or proclaiming the Word of God—in a sermon, for instance—is a type of prophecy because the pastor is explaining the Word of God to the people of God. There's biblical support for this type of prophecy in Luke 1:67–79. In this passage Zechariah was filled with the Holy Spirit and prophesied by explaining and applying the Old Testament Scriptures. The Blue Letter Bible explains, "The content of what he said was not new revelation but rather the announcement that certain promises found in the Old Testament were about to be fulfilled. This prophecy was for the purpose of informing, building up and consoling the people—it was not new truth which had previously been unrevealed."[3]

John Piper, in his sermon titled "The Authority and Nature of the Gift of Prophecy," insightfully compared the gift of teaching with the gift of prophecy.[4] Essentially, his point was that we value the gift of teaching as a gift that can edify the church. At the same time, we recognize that the teacher can be fallible even though the source is not. In other words, the Bible is infallible. The teacher is fallible because of their inability to perfectly interpret and understand the infallible Word of God. But we accept the potential for fallibility in the teacher and therefore are instructed to always test what is taught.

We would all agree that we have benefited significantly from the spiritual gift of teaching. It has edified and always will edify the church, despite the errors that even faithful pastors make. Piper argues that the gift of prophecy should be regarded in the same light. It is not authoritative in the same way the Word of God is. It should not be considered new revelation on par with the Bible (as some traditions teach), but it can be helpful and edifying to the body of Christ just as the spiritual gift of teaching can be. The apostle Paul suggested this in his first letter to the church at Corinth: "The person who prophesies speaks to people for their strengthening, encouragement, and consolation" (1 Corinthians 14:3).

Another question sometimes arises: Should the gift of prophecy be limited to church leaders? Scripture doesn't support that conclusion. Consider Acts 21:9, which describes a man who "had four virgin daughters who prophesied." One view on how the gift of prophecy functions today is espoused by John Piper. He suggests that we need a "new category in our thinking" to help us understand the types of prophets and prophecy that Scripture reveals.

First there are true prophets who are infallible, such as the Old Testament prophets, Jesus, the apostles, and the biblical writers. These prophets were mouthpieces for God Himself and provided *new* revelation. Next there are false prophets, who will be judged severely for their heretical prophecies (more on this later). Then Piper calls for "a third category for the 'spiritual gift of prophecy'—Spirit-prompted, Spirit-sustained, revelation-rooted, but mixed with human imperfection and fallibility and therefore in need of sifting."[5] In the same way in which we would say that a Bible teacher is under the influence of the Spirit yet still needs careful evaluation, it is safe to apply that same mindset to someone who claims to be a prophet.

If the New Testament prophets were infallible, there would have been no need for Paul to command the church to "evaluate" and "test" the prophecies of its members: "Don't despise prophecies, but test all things. Hold on to what is good" (1 Thessalonians 5:20–21).

The assumption here is that there could be some good from prophecies that we should "hold on to," but Paul also introduced the possibility that an entire prophecy might *not* be worth holding on to. He repeated this concept elsewhere: "Two or three prophets should speak, and the others should evaluate" (1 Corinthians 14:29).

It seems that Paul was putting the New Testament gift of prophecy in the same category as the gift of teaching. Here's another related consideration: During the Old Testament age, if someone prophesied falsely in the name of the Lord, God ordered that person to be put to death. We have no such command for the New Testament prophets. Apparently the New Testament gift of prophecy doesn't carry the same authority as the role or office of prophet described in the Old Testament.[6]

Prophecy as New Revelation

Do we see examples of prophecy as new revelation in the New Testament? In other words, are there instances where a prophecy was given but it wasn't written down or considered Scripture for the entire church? We see several examples of this in the New Testament. Consider the prophecy of Agabus in the book of Acts: "One of them, named Agabus, stood up and predicted by the Spirit that there would be a severe famine throughout the Roman world. This took place during the reign of Claudius" (Acts 11:28). This prophecy came to pass exactly as Agabus predicted.

Later he issued a prophecy concerning the apostle Paul: "After we had been there for several days, a prophet named Agabus came down from Judea. He came to us, took Paul's belt, tied his own feet and hands, and said, 'This is what the Holy Spirit says: "In this way the Jews in Jerusalem will bind the man who owns this belt and deliver him over to the Gentiles"'" (Acts 21:10–11). Although the accuracy of a few details is debated, the basics of Agabus's prophecy were fulfilled.

Some also consider Acts 13:1–2 an example of prophecy as new revelation: "Now in the church at Antioch there were prophets and teachers: Barnabas, Simeon who was called Niger, Lucius of Cyrene, Manaen, a close friend of Herod the tetrarch, and Saul. As they were worshiping the Lord and fasting, the Holy Spirit said, 'Set apart for me Barnabas and Saul for the work to which I have called them.'" Notice here that as they were worshiping and fasting, the Holy Spirit gave them instructions that are not found in any written scripture we have today.

Consider also the prophecies spoken over Timothy's life before he went into ministry and was commissioned by the apostle Paul: "Timothy, my son, I am giving you this instruction in keeping with the prophecies previously made about you, so that by recalling them you may fight the good fight, having faith and a good conscience, which some have rejected and have shipwrecked their faith" (1 Timothy 1:18–19).

The Bible Knowledge Commentary explains,

> When and by whom these prophecies were made can only be guessed. It is known that the prophecies reinforced Paul's conviction that Timothy was a fit soldier to conduct the battle against error in the Ephesian church (cf. 6:12; 2 Tim. 4:7 for an athletic rather than military metaphor). Timothy was to remember these prophecies and be inspired by them in the struggle.[7]

The fact that a specific prophecy was spoken over Timothy's life is confirmed in 1 Timothy 4:14: "Don't neglect the gift that is in you; it was given to you through prophecy, with the laying on of hands by the council of elders."

Do I believe that God can use someone to speak a word beyond what's explicitly stated in the Scriptures, a word that can encourage and provide insight and wisdom to a fellow believer? Yes, I do. Do I believe that God is using people today to provide a general authoritative message to the body of Christ as *new revelation* that's not found in the Bible? No, not at all. To assert this would violate the principle of *sola scriptura*: the canon is closed, and Scripture provides all that we need for life and godliness.

> We don't see authoritative new revelation for the entire body of Christ through individual prophets.

We don't see authoritative new revelation for the entire body of Christ through individual prophets. Prophecy today is primarily geared toward *forthtelling* (a Spirit-empowered teaching of God's truth as revealed in the Scriptures) or providing especially insightful words of truth and wisdom that may not be explicitly contained in Scripture but are consistent with it and provide special encouragement to the hearer.

FALSE PROPHETS

Now that we've established the potential that prophecy today can be edifying but not necessarily authoritative for the body of Christ, what does the Bible say about false prophets? And how do we recognize them so that we aren't misled?

First, I want you to see just how seriously God takes it when a mere human being claims to speak on His behalf. This is not something He takes lightly any more than you would if someone presumed to speak on your behalf. God punished the prophets who spoke falsely to the people in His name. This has significant application for today: many Christians use the words "God told me . . ." when speaking prophetically to other people. We'll discuss that a bit later in this chapter, but first let's take a look at what Scripture says about the consequences false prophets faced in the Old Testament.

Perhaps the most central passage demonstrating God's heart toward false prophets is found in the book of Jeremiah:

> "Even the priests and prophets
> are ungodly, wicked men.
> I have seen their despicable acts
> right here in my own Temple,"
> says the LORD.
> "Therefore, the paths they take
> will become slippery.
> They will be chased through the dark,

and there they will fall.

For I will bring disaster upon them

at the time fixed for their punishment.

I, the LORD, have spoken!"

—JEREMIAH 23:11–12 NLT

In verse 14, God delineated exactly what He had against them: "But now I see that the prophets of Jerusalem are even worse! They commit adultery and love dishonesty. They encourage those who are doing evil so that no one turns away from their sins. These prophets are as wicked as the people of Sodom and Gomorrah once were" (Jeremiah 23:14 NLT).

Not only did God call out their hypocritical character but He said they were not fulfilling the most basic responsibility of a prophet, which was to call the people to turn from their sins. In their silence they were actually encouraging the people's sinful behavior. But it gets worse. "This is what the LORD of Heaven's Armies says to his people: 'Do not listen to these prophets when they prophesy to you, filling you with futile hopes. They are making up everything they say. They do not speak for the LORD!'" (Jeremiah 23:16 NLT).

Notice here that God pronounced judgment on these prophets because they were filling people with what He called "futile hopes." This is exactly what we see happening in our culture today. Many so-called prophets are filling people with futile hopes:

"Your breakthrough is on the way."

"Your healing is on the way."

"Your marriage will be restored this year."

"God is going to open up your womb this year."

"God wants to declare to you today that your struggles are over!"

"God is going to bless you financially tenfold!"

Many false prophets are preying on people's desires and promising them things they know those people want to hear. The apostle Paul predicted this would happen as well: "For a time is coming when people will no longer listen to sound and wholesome teaching. They will follow their own desires and will look for teachers who will tell them whatever their itching ears want to hear" (2 Timothy 4:3 NLT).

The time that Paul was referring to is now here.

Returning to Jeremiah, we read, "I have not sent these prophets, yet they run around claiming to speak for me. I have given them no message, yet they go on prophesying" (Jeremiah 23:21 NLT). This is the bottom line: Many of the people who claim to be prophets are not really prophets. They are speaking their own words. Those who do so should heed the warning God gave the false prophets in the Old Testament:

> The prophet who presumes to speak a message in my name that I have not commanded him to speak, or who speaks in the name of other gods—that prophet must die. You may say to yourself, "How can we recognize a message the LORD has not spoken?" When a prophet speaks in the LORD's name, and the message does not come true or is not fulfilled, that is a message the LORD has not spoken. The prophet has spoken it presumptuously. Do not be afraid of him.
>
> —DEUTERONOMY 18:20–22

The penalty for issuing a false prophecy in the Old Testament was death. Thankfully the punishment is not as severe in the New Testament times in which we live. But that doesn't mean God takes it any less seriously when a person presumes to speak on His behalf today.

In the Old Testament, prophets were not only expected to be accurate but they were also to be *specific*. Many of the prophecies we see today are vague and general. In a crowd of two thousand people, comments like "Your marriage will be restored this year" or "Someone here will experience a financial breakthrough next month" could refer to any number of people with broken marriages or broken finances. I would encourage you to pay minimal attention to vague prophecies.

THE "GOD TOLD ME" SYNDROME

Many Christians would never claim to be prophets, since they aren't standing on a stage at a church service, conference, or crusade heralding, "Thus says the Lord." But they often function as prophets when they say three increasingly popular words: "God told me . . ." This is especially true now with the advent of social media sites that give anyone and everyone a platform for claiming they have spiritual authority.

If you hang out in Christian circles long enough, it's inevitable you will hear someone say, "God told me . . ." If God tells a person something through the work of the Holy Spirit that is consistent with God's Word, we can probably conclude that it came from God. Why? Because the Spirit's job is to confirm the written Word of God to the child of God. And what this person is saying has already been revealed as authoritative in the Word. So they are merely reminding someone else of what God has already said.

But what we are talking about here is something called *extra-biblical revelation*. This is when a person claims to hear from God on a matter totally unrelated to the written Word of God. You might hear comments along these lines:

"God told me that man was going to be my husband."
"God showed me in a dream last night that the two of you should marry each other."

"God told me to buy this house."

"God told me to start this business."

"God told me to give this money away."

"God told me to share the message He gave me for you in a dream last night."

"God told me to move to this city."

"God told me to eat at Burger King today even though I was headed to McDonald's."

Okay, that last one was a bit silly, but you get my point, right? There are a number of problems associated with the "God told me" syndrome, but I'll highlight just two.

First, when you come across people who consistently claim to have extrabiblical revelations from God, it's probably because they want others to think they have some private connection with God that others don't have. Being able to hear from God on a regular basis is a spiritual status symbol. It somehow proves they have this intimate relationship with God like Moses did, where God speaks to them about even the most minute matters of life. It invariably makes other Christians who don't hear from God as clearly or consistently feel that their connection with Him isn't as deep or meaningful. Let's be honest. These kinds of claims elevate the person who makes them rather than building up those who are listening.

The second major problem is that, if we're being honest, there is no 100 percent certain way of knowing whether it was truly God speaking or our own thoughts or desires. When I thought God told me to go to Burger King, maybe I was just craving a Whopper more than a Big Mac (even though I don't eat either of those—ha!). Perhaps it would be better to say, "I truly believe it was God who led me to say . . ." By saying it this way, you are humbly introducing the potential of human error. "I truly believe" shows that you understand your revelation very well may not have been God, but as best you can discern, you *believe* it was. Considering how God feels about people who speak on His behalf, I would encourage you to use the words "God told me" sparingly—or even remove them from your vocabulary.

HOW TO TEST A PROPHETIC WORD

This brings us to the most important question in this chapter: How should we as Christians evaluate or respond to prophecy so we can guard against being misled like Jarren? Because I cannot find any scripture that clearly suggests that it's *impossible* for God to use someone to speak wisdom apart from the Word *specifically* into a person's life, I can only conclude that it's possible but should be received with caution. If someone claims to have a prophetic word for us, here are a few tests I suggest you apply to discern whether it truly is a word from God for you.

Test #1: Receive It but Don't Always Believe It

When someone comes to you and says they have a word from God for you, don't be rude or dismissive. Listen to what they have to say but don't immediately receive it as a word from God. "Do not quench the Spirit. Do not despise prophecies, but test everything; hold fast what is good" (1 Thessalonians 5:19–21 ESV).

It seems Paul was suggesting that being quick to despise prophecies could quench or extinguish what the Spirit may want to do. Instead, he instructs us to hold on to what is good. This implies that some good could stem from a prophecy, but it needs to be tested or sifted first. Another key verse is 1 John 4:1 (ESV): "Beloved, do not believe every spirit, but test the spirits to see whether they are from God, for many false prophets have gone out into the world."

Whether someone claims to have a specific word for you or is teaching from the Word of God, John's instruction is the same: If someone says, "I believe God put something on my heart concerning your life," don't immediately turn them away. Doing so would suggest that you don't believe God could use someone else to speak into your life. John instructs us to consider the source. Does this person have a proven track record of being accurate with what they believe God has spoken to them? Do they have a solid grasp on biblical truth? Or are they just a random person who had a dream about you last night?

Test #2: Beware of Vague and General Prophecies

If someone who claims to be a prophet speaks a word of prophecy over your life, look for specificity rather than vague and general words that could apply to many people. When God spoke through a prophet in the Bible, most often it was a very specific word. If it's not, this should immediately raise red flags. Many modern-day prophets have made a living by addressing a crowd of people and pronouncing a vague prophetic word, arousing the hunger and curiosity of all those who attend. The more vague the prophecy is, the higher the likelihood it will apply to someone. The more specific it is, the more risk the prophet takes that no one will publicly acknowledge that the prophecy was for them. When God communicated a message to His people in any form throughout history, it was direct and clearly understood by the intended audience.

Test #3: Scripture Must Always Be the Ultimate Authority

Whenever someone speaks into your life, be sure that the spirit of what they're saying is consistent with the Word of God. Regardless of how good, specific, or accurate a prophecy may sound, human prophecy will never trump the authority of God's Word. If it deviates in any way from what is in the written Word of God, it should be rejected. Paul beautifully illustrated the authority of the Scriptures:

> Now concerning the coming of our Lord Jesus Christ and our being gathered to him: We ask you, brothers and sisters, not to be easily upset or troubled, either by a prophecy or by a message or by a letter supposedly from us, alleging that the day of the Lord has come. Don't let anyone deceive you in any way. For that day will not come unless the apostasy comes first and the man of lawlessness is revealed, the man doomed to destruction.
>
> —2 THESSALONIANS 2:1–3

In this passage, Paul was establishing that his authority as an apostle of Christ superseded any sort of prophecy the people might have been tempted to follow. John Piper explains:

> Now the point is this: Today the New Testament stands where the apostles stood. Their authority is exercised today through their writings and the writings of their close associates like Luke and Mark and James (the Lord's brother). So, in the same way Paul made apostolic teaching the final authority in those days, so we make the apostolic teaching the final authority in our day. That means the New Testament is our authority. And since the New Testament endorses the Old Testament as God's inspired word, we take the whole Bible as our rule and measuring rod of all teachings and all prophecies about what we should believe and how we should live.[8]

Paul also affirmed the priority and primacy of the written Word: "If anyone thinks he is a prophet or spiritual, he should recognize that what I write to you is the Lord's command. If anyone ignores this, he will be ignored" (1 Corinthians 14:37–38).

Notice that Paul was establishing the Bible's authority above and beyond the authority of any self-proclaimed prophet. Don't assume that what someone is saying to you is true just because they claim to be a prophet.

Test #4: Share the Prophecy with Trusted Spiritual Leaders

This test is consistent with Paul's instruction to the church in Corinth: "Two or three prophets should speak, and the others should evaluate" (1 Corinthians 14:29). The "others" who are evaluating the validity of this prophecy are the church leaders. So when someone comes to you with a prophetic word, share it with trusted leaders at your church so they can help you evaluate it.

Test #5: Ask God to Confirm the Prophecy

Finally, because prophecy is considered one of the less reliable ways God speaks to us, ask Him to confirm whatever prophetic word is being spoken over your life so that you aren't making a decision based solely on something that someone said to you.

A HEALTHY BALANCE

So how should we view prophecy today? On one hand we cannot conclude that it is impossible for God to speak to us through another person. There simply isn't enough scriptural support to suggest that. What we *can* conclude is that the majority of self-proclaimed prophets today are probably not functioning the way the Old Testament prophets did. We can determine this by comparing the ministries and messages of many modern-day prophets with the ministries and messages of prophets in the Bible. God will severely discipline those who are guilty of speaking prophetic words on behalf of God that He has not spoken.

I would also suggest eliminating the words "God told me" from your vocabulary unless you are 100 percent certain they came from God. Claiming that God has given you a word for someone else is both dangerous and unnecessary. When you say these three words, the other person feels obligated to believe and follow the prophecy since you claim it was from God. For these reasons, we must conclude that although prophecy can still edify the church, it's one of the less reliable ways God speaks to us.

> **Although prophecy can still edify the church, it's a less reliable way God speaks to us.**

Finally, modern-day prophets should always function according to biblical principles. A prophet should focus primarily on calling out sin, inviting people to repent, warning them of the consequences of sin, and providing specific prophecies. When a prophet is operating in this capacity, they will need to embrace the fact that the vast majority of people will see them in a negative light since they are fulfilling their prophetic responsibility to expose the darkness and deception people are comfortable with. For that reason, they ought to be prepared for a life of sacrifice and surrender rather than a life of popularity and glamour.

FIVE

113

J arren's hopes of finding his ideal church had faded nearly into extinction. Month after month of investment and belief returned only disappointment and disillusionment. And though he didn't like to admit it even to himself, Jarren felt more confused and conflicted now than when he'd started his Christian journey. The joy he'd felt as a new convert had faded, and he struggled not to immerse himself in feeling jaded and disillusioned. He was just about ready to give up on church.

But one afternoon Jarren felt a glimmer of hope. He was having coffee with Skye, an acquaintance from work, when she mentioned that she was a Christian. Unable to resist the chance of connecting, Jarren opened up about the frustrating journey he'd been on.

"I'm so sorry for what you've been going through," Skye said after he finished sharing. Her eyes were full of sympathy. "That is *crazy*. I mean, *really* crazy. But not every church is like that—pressuring you to have certain experiences, or telling you to give lots of money, or pushing a bunch of mumbo jumbo about manifesting your desires. I attend the Love Church across town. Have you ever heard of it?"

"No, I haven't," Jarren replied. *And I'm not sure I want to.* Despite being so weary of the pressure, the judgment, and the letdowns, in an effort to be polite he asked his new friend, "What's it like?"

"It's the most accepting church I've ever been a part of. It's amazing to see people from all walks of life worshiping God together in one room. It's like they accept you no matter who you are or what you're struggling with. No judgment, no pressure—just a place for people who love Jesus and love others."

This was music to Jarren's ears because he was battling—and sometimes giving in to—intense temptation regarding pornography and sexual sin. He needed a church where he wouldn't be reprimanded, challenged, or judged because of his struggles.

"Also, there are no restrictions on who can serve at our church. Everyone is welcome!"

"Wow!" Jarren said, his curiosity starting to rise.

"You should also know that we believe in the Bible and love to study it together, but we recognize that it's an ancient book written for people from cultures that are really different from today's culture. So instead of just reading rules off the page, we recognize that some things might not apply to us now or might apply to us in different ways. My pastor can explain all about it if you come and visit."

Jarren knew that modern-day Christians didn't follow certain parts of the Old Testament anymore, so this didn't sound alarming. "Why not?" he said. "I'll give it a try." And sure enough, he found the Love Church vastly different from the other churches he had attended—but he loved it. In the chairs next to him were openly gay couples, trans people, and others he hadn't seen in previous churches. *This church finally gets it! I mean, if we're going to reach these groups, they have to feel comfortable here. Why didn't I see these types of people at all of the other churches I visited before? Church is where they need to be!*

But as time went on and Jarren learned more of the details and nuances of what the Love Church believed, red flags started to give him pause. He noticed that everyone had a dramatically different view of Jesus from the one he'd been taught. To many, Jesus was just another man—a very good man whose example we should follow, but not actually God. Jarren also discovered why people who weren't following traditional Christian teachings about gender and sexuality felt so comfortable at the Love Church. They weren't just accepted into the fellowship; they were taught that traditional understandings of sex, marriage, and family were either misinterpretations of the Bible or were no longer applicable.

Jarren also noticed that the pastor never mentioned sin. He encouraged people to remain in whatever lifestyle they were in when they came. Gay, lesbian, and trans people were in leadership positions, doing the announcements, and teaching classes—but something didn't sit right for Jarren. In fact, he felt discouraged.

He'd initially enjoyed going to a church that accepted him the way he was without making him feel judged (or even remotely uncomfortable!) about his own lifestyle choices. But he also knew there were things he needed to change—and he wasn't being challenged or helped to make any of those changes. Even after listening to the pastor and other church leaders explain their views, Jarren felt pretty sure from his own reading of the Bible that his use of pornography and occasionally having sex with his girlfriend didn't match up with biblical standards. Was this church's attitude of loving acceptance really just based on dismissing what the Bible seemed to clearly teach?

What initially felt like relief became a burden, especially as Jarren battled the negative consequences of his own lifestyle. The emotional toll of his sexually active dating relationship—not to mention what was beginning to feel like an addiction to pornography—left him yearning for some accountability. He even found himself missing some good old-fashioned calls to repentance and holiness!

He knew something was really wrong when he heard the pastor affirm two men who wanted to adopt a child. Then the pastor affirmed a woman's right to have an abortion. Even before he became a believer, Jarren had a high regard for human life, and Christianity had solidified that belief. So when he heard the pastor support abortion, his heart broke. His hopes of finding a church were dashed once again. And he felt more confused than ever about the gospel, Jesus, and what it meant to live as a Christian.

WHAT IS PROGRESSIVE CHRISTIANITY?

Jarren encountered a brand of Christianity today called *progressive Christianity*. It's not an official organization or denomination but rather an active movement of self-identified Christians and Christian groups characterized by a collection of beliefs and attitudes that set them apart from traditional Christianity. One of the major effects of this movement is the gradual erosion of traditional Christian teachings, which calls into question whether progressive Christianity can be called "Christian" in any meaningful sense.

> A major effect of progressive Christianity is the gradual erosion of traditional Christian teachings.

This chapter focuses on preparing you to defend historical Christian beliefs when you encounter proponents of progressive Christianity. First I'll share a brief history of the movement and expose some of its core tenets so you can identify them. Then we'll discuss how the Bible refutes the false teachings progressive Christians espouse. And as always, we'll end with striking a healthy and balanced perspective on progressive Christianity.

Before we jump in, however, I want to emphasize that although I use the terms *progressive Christians* and *progressive Christianity* throughout the chapter, I don't endorse this movement as Christian in any sense of the word. As we'll see, its core tenets deviate from biblical Christian beliefs to such an extent that I don't believe we can consider it a valid branch of Christianity.

HOW PROGRESSIVE CHRISTIANITY GOT STARTED

The origins of progressive Christianity are complex. The movement embraces some aspects of liberal Christianity, which can be traced back to both Enlightenment-era rationalism and the Romanticism of the eighteenth and nineteenth centuries. While progressive Christianity shares some features of the social gospel movement of the late nineteenth and early twentieth centuries, it can also be seen as a reaction against it. The term *progressive Christianity* arose in the early 1990s with the founding of the Center for Progressive Christianity. A wide range of people claim to be progressive Christians. They don't always agree with each other, but they do tend to share a similar set of attitudes and beliefs, which we'll identify later.

Roots in Postmodernism

The general idea behind the progressive Christian movement is that the church needs to revisit and adjust its methods, practices, and beliefs as the culture changes. This approach was largely borrowed from postmodernism. What is postmodernism, you ask? Maybe the easiest way to answer that question is to compare it with modernism.

The modernism of the eighteenth and nineteenth centuries focused on rational inquiry and empirical evidence. Modernists were highly optimistic that science and philosophy could unlock any mystery and explain just about everything. Postmodernism is a reaction against that optimism. Here's a handy set of contrasts:

- Modernists asserted that everyone had direct, reliable access to reality and the ability to obtain knowledge; postmodernists argue that everyone's perception of reality is radically and inescapably limited by their cultural context and individual perspectives.
- Modernists thought people could discover and understand

timeless, universal truths; postmodernists believe that truth is relative, varying from situation to situation, from culture to culture, and even from individual to individual.

- Modernists looked for a metanarrative, a grand, overarching story that explained how the world works; postmodernists reject even the possibility of a metanarrative, choosing instead to celebrate the idea that any culture or individual can craft their own narrative to create their own meaning and purpose.
- Modernists saw universal truth and reason as paths toward the advancement and betterment of humankind; postmodernists are suspicious of any claim to universal truth or reason and claim that objective truth is just a power play in disguise, an attempt to control and oppress others.

No wonder a pessimistic and suspicious mood began to take over in the wake of the Second World War! Postmodernism initially found footholds in the mid-1900s in the academic disciplines of philosophy, art, and literature, but it didn't take long to filter into the popular consciousness.

You probably recognize some of the progressive ideas I summarized. Have you ever heard people talk about "my truth" or "your truth," as if truth is little more than an individual opinion? That's postmodernism talking. Have you ever noticed that tolerance and open-mindedness are lifted up as the highest virtues, while people who claim certainty (especially about morality) are treated with suspicion or even shouted down? That's postmodernism talking too.

The Emergent Church and Progressive Christianity

Early versions of progressive Christianity initially took root in the more theologically and culturally liberal parts of the Protestant church, where traditional Christian teachings were already being

WHAT DOES PROGRESSIVE CHRISTIANITY TEACH?

challenged or rejected. But in the early 2000s, a phenomenon known as the Emergent Church began to gain influence in evangelical circles and laid the groundwork for today's progressive Christianity.

Let's take a moment to recognize the good points postmodernism makes, at least in terms of what it was reacting against. Modernism's quest for certainty in all things was an overreach—a healthy dose of intellectual humility is a good thing. And modernism's emphasis on our ability to grasp universal truth wasn't just about the joy of intellectual discovery; in some cases it led to increasingly horrifying abuses of scientific knowledge and power that caused massive human suffering.

So maybe it's not such a surprise that many in the Emergent Church saw postmodernism as a helpful corrective. Shouldn't we embrace a humble recognition that we're limited creatures, incapable of knowing and understanding everything? Isn't it right to treat other people and cultures with respect? Isn't it good to be filled with awe at the incalculable mystery of God and His amazing creation instead of thinking we've got it all figured out? Many evangelicals in the early 2000s resonated with the Emergent Church movement's emphasis on holy mystery over highly systematized doctrines, spiritual openness over intellectual certainty, and seemingly humble curiosity over self-satisfied traditionalism.

But the postmodern cure turned out to be worse than the disease of modernism, or at least caused a different kind of sickness. The fact that the Emergent Church movement failed to affirm any sort of official statement of faith should have been a warning sign. In 2006 Emergent leader Tony Jones published this comment by LeRon Shults:

Emergent aims to facilitate a conversation among persons committed to living out faithfully the call to participate in the reconciling mission of the biblical God . . . A "statement of faith" tends to stop conversation. . . . Too often they create an environment in which real conversation is avoided out of fear that critical reflection on one or more of the sacred propositions will lead to excommunication from the community.[1]

Do you see what Shults is suggesting? In short, he's saying, "Let's move away from focusing on truth and conversations about what the church believes—because we want to make people feel comfortable voicing their doubts and questions without fear of being rejected by their community." This reveals several hallmarks of the Emergent movement: prioritizing conversation over conclusions, valuing asking questions over claiming to have answers, and emphasizing the idea that doubt is healthy and compatible with faith—largely because it drives the process of questioning and staying engaged in conversation.

But the warning signs didn't end there. Postmodernism rejected not only the idea that we can know the truth but even the notion that absolute truth exists at all. And it wasn't long before the Emergent Church followed suit, directing that attitude of skepticism and suspicion toward Christian doctrines. My friend and colleague Alisa Childers writes, "Along with reexamining the methods of the church, some influential emergent thinkers began to reexamine the beliefs and doctrines of historic Christianity. No longer were they questioning only methods, traditions, practices and philosophical approaches; they were also casting doubt on essential Christian doctrines themselves."[2]

And so through the Emergent movement, progressive Christianity took root within many evangelical circles and opened the door for Christians to start reinterpreting the Bible, rethinking long-held teachings, and even questioning fundamental Christian doctrines and dogma.[3]

Opening the Door to Deconstruction

You can imagine the impact this had on the culture. When Christians began questioning what they believed (which is not necessarily a bad thing), many of them had neither the tools nor the community to correctly process their historic Christian beliefs. The result? Many Christians began a process called *deconstruction*.

There's plenty of debate about exactly how to define this term. Some claim that deconstruction is really just a healthy (though sometimes difficult) process of reevaluating inherited beliefs, working through doubts and questions, and eventually rebuilding a more genuine faith. Let me say this clearly: If you grew up in a church that caused spiritual or emotional damage, or if you inherited some form of cultural Christianity without making it your own, you may *need* to reexamine your faith. It may be difficult and painful, but it's important that your faith is genuine. I hope and pray that you will grow in your faith while breaking free from any harm or abuse you may have experienced from churches in your past. As I shared at the beginning of the book, I myself had to work through that process. But that's not the kind of deconstruction I'm talking about—and I would argue that *deconstruction* isn't the best term to use in describing a healthy reevaluation of your faith.

> If you inherit cultural Christianity without making it your own, you may *need* to reexamine your faith.

What I'm concerned about is the kind of deconstruction that can result from progressive Christianity's tendency to undermine both Scripture and the core tenets of the faith. The writers at Got Questions define *deconstruction* this way: "'Deconstruction' is . . . the process of questioning, doubting, and ultimately rejecting aspects of Christian faith."[4]

Don't Be Surprised . . .

It shouldn't catch any Bible-reading Christian off guard that progressive Christianity is leading people away from true Christianity using

Christian terms and biblical phrases to promote a false gospel. Jesus and the New Testament writers predicted this would occur. The apostle Paul said, "Now the Spirit explicitly says that in later times some will depart from the faith, paying attention to deceitful spirits and the teachings of demons" (1 Timothy 4:1). And Jesus said, "Be on your guard against false prophets who come to you in sheep's clothing but inwardly are ravaging wolves. . . . Many false prophets will rise up and deceive many" (Matthew 7:15; 24:11).

Both Jesus and the New Testament writers prophesied that false prophets who appear to be fellow Christians will deceive and mislead many people. And that is exactly what we see happening with progressive Christianity.

WHAT PROGRESSIVE CHRISTIANITY TEACHES

Let's examine five of the most dangerous tendencies that characterize progressive Christianity. To be fair, some who identify as progressive Christians hold views that diverge from what is presented here, but I think these five tendencies characterize the beliefs of the majority. This movement can be alluring because it uses familiar biblical and theological terms and often aligns with the most powerful temptations in our culture. It's all too easy to slip into believing this false gospel if you're not equipped beforehand. My hope is that by helping you get a handle on these five tendencies, you'll be able to recognize and stand against teachings that undermine the gospel and lead many astray.

Tendency #1: A Low View of Christ

Some in progressive Christian circles still hold to a traditional understanding that Jesus is fully human and fully God, but a low view of Christ is common. In the words of Dr. Michael Kruger,

One of the hallmarks of progressive Christianity is the way they view Jesus. The orthodox view of Jesus, of course, is that he's the divine Son of God and worthy of our worship and worthy of our adoration and to be praised as God. But, of course, that's not what progressive Christians believe. They believe that Jesus isn't so much the divine Son of God, but rather just a moral example for us to follow. Jesus is more of a big brother that sets a pattern that we walk in his footsteps. That's partly true, of course, we do follow Jesus' example, but progressive Christians make that the main thing. Jesus is just a picture of what we can be and what we can do and his main point is just to set an example for us. The lowering of Jesus is the first mark of progressive Christianity.[5]

A progressive church named Bethel Congregational United Church of Christ confirms this low view of Jesus. Their website says, "Jesus' life, death and resurrection provide the inspiration and challenge for us to live as followers of Jesus today."[6] Another progressive church describes Jesus this way: "The earthly Jesus was a Spirit-filled, first century Jew who embodied the presence of God in his own life and ministry, and is therefore our guide and inspiration for a life dedicated to God."[7]

Writing for ProgressiveChristianity.org, Carl Krieg says this about Jesus:

When we look at Jesus in relation to his disciples, instead of looking at the "person and work" of Jesus, we look at who he was in relational encounter. We thereby avoid the Chalcedonian problems of trying to relate his divinity and his humanity. He was able to impact others because he was a true human being. It was the fullness of his humanity that enabled others to see in him what they also could become and were meant to be. . . . Jesus was the perfect human who was also the perfect window to God. It's not as though there was a divine nature in him, but rather that his fully human nature was transparent to the God who inheres all reality.[8]

These clear rejections of the deity of Jesus immediately disqualify such groups from being truly Christian in any meaningful sense. For one thing, Jesus Himself claimed to be divine. From its earliest days the Christian church recognized those claims. And while it may have taken the church many years and lots of conversations to fully articulate Jesus' full humanity and full divinity, there's always been a strong consensus that the divinity of Jesus is an indispensable cornerstone of the faith.

If you ever hear a pastor brushing aside or de-emphasizing the divinity of Jesus, that's a huge red flag. And if you'd like to dig into why the divinity of Jesus matters for the gospel, take a look at the list of recommended resources at the back of this book.

Tendency #2: Inclusivism

Progressive Christianity prides itself on accepting and loving people from all walks of life. On the surface this appears to be consistent with what the Scriptures teach regarding how we should engage with the outside world.

While the first tendency (a low view of Christ) is widespread, it's not universal in progressive Christianity. But I think the principle of inclusivism is practically a universal dogma within the movement and is regularly lifted up as one of their core beliefs. In their own words, they "seek community that is inclusive of all people, honoring differences in theological perspectives, age, race, sexual orientation, gender identity/expression, class, or ability."[9]

This emphasis on inclusivity is rooted in how they define love. Progressive Christianity puts a significant emphasis, and rightly so, on the importance of loving our neighbors and our enemies. This sounds a lot like Jesus, doesn't it? But that's only part of the picture. On Bethel's website, they state the following: "We believe that Jesus' commandment to 'love one another as I have loved you' is foundational. . . . Further, love of neighbor includes *affirmation* of the LBGTQ community, immigrants, people of other faith traditions and even those who are enemies."[10]

We see here that progressive Christianity equates love with affirmation. Furthermore, their inclusivism extends beyond accepting and affirming people from various walks of life to affirming the beliefs and practices of various religions. While we should welcome people from all religions into our homes, communities, and churches, we should not go so far as to affirm that other religions are just as true as Christianity or equally valid paths to salvation. But this is exactly what progressive Christianity teaches.

The Christian faith is our way of being faithful to God. But it is not the only way. Christianity is the truth for us. But it is not the only truth. This principle stems from the reality of the 21st century. We share our lives with people who are Muslim, Jewish, Hindu, Buddhist. We experience these people as loving and caring by following their religious traditions. To deny that is to [insist] that God can only draw people with one way. That simply isn't born out in our experience.

The power of the Christian faith to transform lives does not require it to be exclusively true. Exclusivity is born out of fear. The fear that there is one train to God and if you aren't on the right train, you'll go to hell. We believe there are many trains and God welcomes them all.[11]

> "We believe there are many trains and God welcomes them all."

Within the first few sentences we run into a serious problem. It's the proverbial "it's true for me but not for you" argument. We'll explore the error of this thinking in our biblical analysis of this second tendency. But suffice it to say that the principle of inclusivism is what happens when the Christian principle of loving our neighbor is blended with and warped by the postmodern insistence on uncertainty and relativism.

Tendency #3: A Low View of Scripture

Progressive Christianity, along with the other false doctrines presented in this book, claims the Bible as the source of their beliefs and practices: "The Bible is read at every one of our progressive Christian worship services and is the foundation of our beliefs, faith, and values."[12] Again, sounds pretty good, right?

But while the Bible may be read at their services, progressive Christians generally have a low regard for Scripture's authority for Christians today. Alisa Childers sums up their view of the Scriptures well:

> In the progressive church, the Bible is viewed more like an ancient spiritual travel journal than the inspired, inerrant, and authoritative Word of God. The Biblical writers are viewed as well-meaning ancient people who were doing their best to understand God in the times and places in which they lived, but they were not necessarily speaking for God. Scripture is also seen as contradictory, not internally coherent, and not authoritative for Christians.[13]

It would certainly be wrong for us to simply take her or any other Christian's word on what another group believes. So let's look at what progressive Christian churches say about how they regard the Bible. Pay close attention to the language used.

For example, look at BeLOVEd Way's statement regarding the Bible. The first warning sign is that the header simply says, "New Testament Is Our Guide."[14] Right away we have two major concerns. First, what about the Old Testament? And second, defining the New Testament as a guide says far too little about the Bible's status and significance. The Bible is composed of both the Old and New Testaments and it is the Word of God, containing timeless truth and final authority on every matter it discusses. A further reading of that church's statement confirms those concerns: they consistently deprioritized the Old Testament and treated the Bible as something less than the final authority in matters of belief and practice.

Here is a heartbreaking description from a progressive congregation called Parkview United Church of Christ: "We take the Bible too seriously to take it literally. We believe that scripture is to be continually interpreted across time, based on the always evolving scholarship in biblical criticism and the unfolding knowledge of the relationship between culture, revelation, experience, tradition, and the witness of the Scriptures."[15]

Are you starting to see a trend? The Bible is not inspired—or "God-breathed" as the Bible describes itself (2 Timothy 3:16)—but merely useful for inspiration. It's useful to begin conversation about things such as marriage, love, money, but it's not the authority on those matters. According to that progressive church, the Bible must be interpreted in light of the evolving culture and experience.

Tendency #4: A Relaxed View of Moral Issues

Progressive Christianity takes a much more relaxed and accepting view of certain behaviors that have historically been viewed as sinful or immoral. Having already demoted the Bible to an inspiring but nonauthoritative document, progressive churches have cleared the way for the belief that humanity's understanding of moral issues has "progressed" over time. While ancient cultures may have seen various behaviors as sinful (with those outdated attitudes reflected in what the movement views as the flawed Scriptures), progressive Christianity claims that we are not necessarily bound by those moral values today. In short, progressive Christianity allows the culture rather than the Bible to dictate what is moral and immoral. Let's look at a couple of the most common issues.

Progressive Christianity's Stance on LGBTQ+

Most progressive churches are Open and Affirming (ONA). An understanding of both terms is critical to get to the heart of what these churches teach and practice. Being *open* means that they are welcoming of those in the LGBTQ+ community. This is not where the problem lies. Every church should want to reach those who are in sin and should thus be open to having them attend. The problem lies with the second term, *affirming*. This is where we get into some trouble. Not only are progressive churches *open* to having LGBTQ+ people visit and attend, but they believe in "affirming the full inclusion of gay, lesbian, bisexual, transgender and non-binary persons (LGBTQ) in the church's life and ministry."[16]

The justifications for this stance in progressive Christian circles are varied and complex. But the following statement I found on one progressive church's website is fairly representative:

> From our perspective, Biblical descriptions of "homosexuality" refer to unhealthy abusive acts that dehumanize. This is in marked contrast to mutually loving, caring, monogamous, healthy, mature relationships between consenting adults who are homosexual, bisexual, and transgendered. . . . We believe that love is a gift from God. When it is shared between two people, in a faithful, intentional relationship, God smiles and says, "It is good."[17]

In other words, homosexuality is wrong only if it involves abuse. But it is acceptable and should be celebrated (since God celebrates it) when it's between two people who express the gift of love toward each other. We'll address the biblical problems with such a stance later in this chapter. But you can see once again how the low view of Scripture is a linchpin that opens the door for redefining just about anything that Christians have traditionally believed or valued.

Progressive Christianity's Stance on Abortion

Progressive Christians, by and large, are pro-choice. In other words, they believe in a woman's right to terminate a pregnancy. Shortly before *Roe v. Wade* was overturned, ProgressiveChristianity.org included this statement on abortion:

> The right to abortion is the mother of all rights. So we must understand this pending decision as an attack on democracy. A woman has a natural right to "vote" for herself on whether or not to continue a pregnancy. Taking away her abortion rights is taking away her voting rights.
>
> If you are against abortion, then don't have one. It is that simple. You can be anti-abortion and pro-choice. You just can't impose your religious beliefs on the rest of us. Especially when for many progressive Christians, reproductive choice is integral to our faith. Our choice-making nature is sacred, God-given. An attack on our reproductive rights is an attack on our religion.
>
> Which is why it is time for our progressive churches to declare ourselves publicly as "Choice Sanctuaries"—where we actively support each other in exercising our sacred human right to reproductive freedom. "Choice Sanctuary" congregations can take on a variety of tasks: helping women get medication abortions, operating an "underground railroad" to other states where "Choice Sanctuary"

churches will help them through their abortions, and of course advocating politically for the full restoration of reproductive rights.[18]

There is a lot to unpack here, but the gist is clear.

Christians have long understood that abortion is the murder of the unborn. One of the earliest Christian writings outside the Bible, the Didache (believed to have been written somewhere between AD 70 and AD 100) says, "You shall not murder a child by abortion."[19] It doesn't get much clearer than that. But progressive Christianity claims that the choice to murder a baby is "integral to our faith." They equate murdering an unborn child with a woman voting for herself. They even claim that God wants them to have the choice to do this. And shockingly, faced with the prospect of *Roe v. Wade* being overturned, they state that they will help "women get medication abortions" and facilitate an "underground railroad" to other states to help mothers access abortions.

Tendency #5: A Rejection of the Atonement

Perhaps the most dangerous tendency of progressive Christians is their rejection of the atoning work of Jesus on the cross. Earlier I wrote about their low view of the *person* of Jesus, failing to recognize His divinity. Now we'll focus on their low view of the *work* of Jesus.

One progressive church describes the atonement this way:

The Divine Spirit effects change or transformation in individuals and communities of faith in many different ways: enlightenment, forgiveness, wholeness, healing, reconciliation, peace, restoration, freedom, and a home coming. The death of Jesus Christ on a cross is seen as an expression of divine self-giving love and not as a sacrifice needed to gain approval or forgiveness by God. Jesus' life, faith and ministry is a model for all to follow.[20]

Notice their emphasis on the external change of the individual through following Jesus' example rather than the eternal salvation of the individual through Jesus' death and resurrection. It's a subtle distinction, but there's a huge difference. Many people throughout history have effected "change or transformation in individuals" through "enlightenment, forgiveness, wholeness" and so on. Some would say that about Oprah Winfrey, Mahatma Gandhi, or the Dalai Lama. This description doesn't distinguish the work of Jesus from the work of any other humanitarian, teacher, or leader.

But it gets worse. Jesus' death is said to be simply the ultimate picture of self-giving love, His way of expressing a divine characteristic. He died as an example to inspire us, "not as a sacrifice needed to gain approval or forgiveness by God." There it is. It doesn't get plainer than that. Progressives do not see what Jesus did on the cross as achieving God's forgiveness for our sin but rather as "a model for all to follow."

RESPONDING TO PROGRESSIVE CHRISTIANITY

Now that we understand some of the main tendencies of progressive Christianity, let's examine each of them according to Scripture.

1. A Biblical Response to the Low View of Christ

A quote we looked at earlier captures the essence of progressive Christianity's stance on Jesus: "Jesus' life, death and resurrection provide the inspiration and challenge for us to live as followers of Jesus today."[21]

Like many of the false teachings examined in this book, there is a hint of truth to this statement. Jesus' life and death *do* provide a challenge for us to follow today. We are to emulate the selfless, moral, and upright life Jesus lived. We are to serve others in our relationships.

But we cannot stop there. A statement like this is not incorrect but rather incomplete. The historic Christian view is that the purpose of Jesus' life, death, and resurrection extends far beyond merely providing an example for us to follow. If this were all Jesus came for, He would be reduced to just another good teacher or moral figure we should emulate.

But what does the Bible say about why Jesus came? In short, it places a different and much greater focus on why Jesus came. As we examine the following verses, note that while Jesus' life is an example for us to follow, the focus is on the atoning nature of His life and death. God gave us His Son so that we might have eternal life, not just so that we would live a better life here on earth.

> When Jesus heard this, he told them, "It is not those who are well who need a doctor, but those who are sick. I didn't come to call the righteous, but sinners."
>
> —MARK 2:17

> "For even the Son of Man did not come to be served, but to serve, and to give his life as a ransom for many."
>
> —MARK 10:45

> "For God loved the world in this way: He gave his one and only Son, so that everyone who believes in him will not perish but have eternal life."
>
> —JOHN 3:16

> "I came into this world for judgment, in order that those who do not see will see and those who do see will become blind."
>
> —JOHN 9:39

This saying is trustworthy and deserving of full acceptance: "Christ Jesus came into the world to save sinners"—and I am the worst of them.

—1 TIMOTHY 1:15

Therefore, he had to be like his brothers and sisters in every way, so that he could become a merciful and faithful high priest in matters pertaining to God, to make atonement for the sins of the people.

—HEBREWS 2:17

For we do not have a high priest who is unable to sympathize with our weaknesses, but one who has been tempted in every way as we are, yet without sin.

—HEBREWS 4:15

But now he has appeared one time, at the end of the ages, for the removal of sin by the sacrifice of himself.

—HEBREWS 9:26

Because Jesus came and experienced what we experience, He is able to understand our weaknesses and advocate on our behalf to the Father—but His sinlessness sets Him apart from every other human and lays the foundation for His vital atoning work on our behalf. Jesus came to call sinners to repentance. He came to redeem those who are lost. And by His own admission Jesus came into the world to judge. This flies in the face of progressive Christianity's avoidance of any kind of judgmental behavior or attitude.

Paul emphasized, as progressive Christianity does, that Jesus is fully human, but he also made it clear that before Jesus was human, He was (and remains) fully divine:

Adopt the same attitude as that of Christ Jesus, who, existing in the form of God, did not consider equality with God as something to be exploited. Instead he emptied himself by assuming the form of a servant, taking on the likeness of humanity. And when he had come as a man, he humbled himself by becoming obedient to the point of death—even to death on a cross.

—Philippians 2:5–8

In other words, Jesus came to demonstrate what true humility, servanthood, and sacrifice look like, and we are commanded to follow His example. But Paul also emphasized Jesus' divine status, using phrases like "existing in the form of God" and "equality with God" to highlight the astonishing sacrifice and humility that God the Son displayed when He assumed (or took on) humanity and came to earth "as a man."

While it is true that Jesus came as an example for us to follow, this is only one of *many* reasons why He came. But progressive Christians choose to focus on the one reason that does *not* distinguish Jesus from other religious leaders.

2. A Biblical Response to Inclusivism

On the surface, inclusivism sounds like an excellent ideal for any Christian. I mean, wasn't Jesus inclusive of all groups? Didn't He accept and embrace and love the social outcasts and marginalized? Well, it depends on how you define the word *accept*. The major difference between how Jesus engaged these groups and how progressive Christianity engages them has to do with the ultimate goal of the engagement.

Jesus' purpose when engaging any group was to expose them to the truth and radically change their lives so they could find freedom from their sinful lifestyles and grow in sanctification. This doesn't appear to be the main goal of the progressive Christian movement. Rather, its proponents not only accept members who openly identify as gay, bisexual, homosexual, or transexual but they accept their lifestyles as well! It is a "come as you are, stay as you are" mentality. This is contrary to the overall mission of Christ. What we see in the gospels are people whose lives were radically changed as they engaged Jesus. Here are just a few examples.

The Sexually Immoral Woman

In Luke 7 a woman who was well known for her sexual immorality disrupted a dinner that a Pharisee was hosting for Jesus. When Jesus engaged her, He didn't simply say, "I embrace you and accept you the way you are." Rather, he publicly called her out for her sin and set her on a path of sanctification. "'Therefore I tell you, her many sins have been forgiven; that's why she loved much. But the one who is forgiven little, loves little.' Then he said to her, 'Your sins are forgiven.' . . . And he said to the woman, 'Your faith has saved you. Go in peace'" (Luke 7:47–48, 50).

Jesus acknowledged that her previous behavior was sinful but offered her forgiveness and peace.

Zacchaeus the Tax Collector

Zacchaeus is another example of someone Jesus challenged yet embraced. As a chief tax collector, Zacchaeus had a history of swindling honest people out of their money by collecting more taxes for the Roman government than were actually owed. In this way he padded his own pockets and was able to live an affluent life. This story is a bit different from the previous one in that Jesus never called out Zacchaeus. But because of his encounter with Christ, Zacchaeus decided to give up his sinful lifestyle. "But Zacchaeus stood there and said to the Lord, 'Look, I'll give half of my possessions to the poor, Lord. And if I have extorted anything from anyone, I'll pay back four times as much'" (Luke 19:8).

Zacchaeus showed true repentance and Jesus commended him for it: "'Today salvation has come to this house,' Jesus told him, 'because he too is a son of Abraham'" (verse 9). Once again, we see a radical change in the lives of those Jesus engaged.

The Rich Young Ruler

In Mark 10 a rich young ruler came to Jesus and asked, "Good teacher, what must I do to inherit eternal life?" (verse 17). After some back and forth, Jesus challenged him to sell his possessions and give the proceeds to the poor. As an aside, this is not meant as a precedent for every believer. Jesus was challenging *this* young man to get rid of the false god of money in his life and allow Jesus to be his true God. Notice the context of Jesus' challenge: "Looking at him, Jesus loved him and said to him, 'You lack one thing: Go, sell all you have and give to the poor, and you will have treasure in heaven. Then come, follow me'" (verse 21).

Jesus genuinely *loved* this young man. But progressive Christians define love as accepting others the way they are and giving them freedom to remain that way. This is not the biblical definition of love. Before moving on, let's see how the young man responded to Jesus' loving challenge: "But he was dismayed by this demand, and he went away grieving, because he had many possessions" (Mark 10:22).

> Progressive Christians define love as accepting others the way they are and giving them freedom to remain that way.

Here is an example of a man whose life was not changed when he encountered Christ. But it wasn't because Jesus accepted him the way he was without challenging him to change. It was because this man wasn't *willing* to change. Significantly for the present discussion, Jesus was not willing to bend His standard of holiness to fit the lifestyle of this man who was in desperate need of repentance.

The Pharisees

The Pharisees were revered as spiritual guides in first-century Judaism. They were responsible for interpreting the law of God for the people of God. Jesus loved them and accepted them but certainly didn't shy away from challenging their hypocrisy. In Matthew 23 we see a courageous encounter Jesus had with them: "Woe to you, scribes and Pharisees, hypocrites! You are like whitewashed tombs, which appear beautiful on the outside, but inside are full of the bones of the dead and every kind of impurity" (Matthew 23:27).

Wow! Jesus did not hold back with these guys. He hit them with the truth, challenging them to repent of their hypocrisy. Clearly, Christlike inclusivism does not mean welcoming everyone into our churches or groups with no loving intention of challenging them to change. It means the opposite. We welcome them the way they are, but we also help them experience sanctification and equip them to forsake the sinful lifestyles or behaviors they are engaged in.

We also noted earlier that progressive Christians are inclusive of other religious beliefs, even though these religions strongly deviate from the Christian worldview. Let's analyze their rationale. Returning to the comments on Bethel's website, we read, "We share our lives with people who are Muslim, Jewish, Hindu, Buddhist. We experience these people as loving and caring by following their religious traditions. To deny that is to [insist] that God can only draw people with one way. That simply isn't born out in our experience."[22]

Their rationale for inclusivity is that since people from other religions are able to express love and care "by following their religious traditions," they demonstrate that they have a genuine relationship with God. This seems to suggest that treating people with love and care proves that members of these other religious groups have had an encounter with the one true God.

The first and most obvious problem here is that treating people with love, dignity, and respect is not, never has been, or ever will be *absolute* proof of one's encounter with God. Atheists can treat people with love and care, and they don't believe in God. The reality is that progressive Christians don't want to tell people of other faiths the truth about their need for Christ and risk offending them when they are exhibiting Christlike character but rejecting Christ. Yet Jesus told us the truth about Himself: "I am the way, the truth, and the life. No one comes to the Father except through me" (John 14:6).

We cannot read this verse and come away with any other conclusion than this: When it comes to pathways to God, Christianity is an exclusive religion, not an inclusive one. There are no trains that get you to God other than the Jesus train.

The heart of the problem with the inclusivism of progressive Christians is their understanding of love. As I pointed out earlier, they define love as accepting people the way they are and giving them freedom to remain that way. But the Bible doesn't define it that way. Time after time Jesus expressed His love through service, sacrifice, and suffering, but He was also bold enough to confront people with the truth of their sinfulness and need for repentance. Any definition of love that falls short of Jesus' example is an inadequate definition or expression of biblical love.

3. A Biblical Response to the Low View of Scripture

A mistake that many well-meaning Christians make is picking and choosing which parts of the Bible they want to accept or reject. They treat the Bible like a buffet, taking what they want and leaving what doesn't taste good to them. For instance, they may embrace the high biblical ideal of loving others but reject passages about sexual sin or repentance. Why? Because those passages force them to deal with their own sin.

That's a temptation for all of us. The principles in the Word of God go against the grain of what our flesh wants to do. So we are left with two choices: either we align our lives with what the Word of God says or we have to find a way to water it down so we can feel better about our sinfulness.

Progressive Christianity largely does the latter. Instead of challenging people to conform to the image of Christ, they disregard the authority of the Word of God and accept lifestyles that contradict what the Bible teaches. Interestingly, the Bible itself affirms its source and authority: "All Scripture is inspired by God and is profitable for teaching, for rebuking, for correcting, for training in righteousness, so that the man of God may be complete, equipped for every good work" (2 Timothy 3:16–17).

First, this passage refers to "all Scripture." This is extremely important considering that when Paul wrote his letter to Timothy, he didn't have a completed New Testament. So this means he was primarily referring to the Old Testament and, by extension, future New Testament writings. Progressive Christians who disregard the authority of the Old Testament are also disregarding the New Testament they claim to revere.

Next it says that the Scriptures are "inspired by God." The Greek word for "inspired" means "God-breathed."[23] While humans penned the actual words of Scripture, their words were God-breathed. Peter affirmed this when he wrote, "Above all, you know this: No prophecy of Scripture comes from the prophet's own interpretation, because no prophecy ever came by the will of man; instead, men spoke from God as they were carried along by the Holy Spirit" (2 Peter 1:20–21).

Men didn't think up Scripture and write it down. They were "carried along by the Holy Spirit." The words they recorded were inspired by God Himself. This is ultimately why the Bible is "profitable for doctrine, for reproof, for correction, for instruction in righteousness" (2 Timothy 3:16 NKJV). Warren Wiersbe explained it like this: "*Doctrine* tells us what is right, *reproof* tells us what is not right, *correction* tells us how to get right, and *instruction* tells us how to stay right."[24] Progressive Christians tend to be selective about when they apply reproof and correction based on their own definitions of what is sinful. But the Bible warns us about this. The apostle Paul affirmed the importance of preaching the *entire* Word of God and not just parts of it: "For I have not shunned to declare to you the whole counsel of God" (Acts 20:27 NKJV).

The Bible forbids us from cherry-picking verses here and there that fit the lifestyles we want to live. We are called not only to observe the entire Word of God but to communicate it in our preaching and teaching. I see progressive Christians erring in both categories—not through mere oversight but blatantly, intentionally, and systematically.

4. A Biblical Response to the Relaxed View of Moral Issues

Earlier in this chapter, we discussed the relaxed moral view of progressive Christianity regarding LGBTQ+ relationships. You may ask how they justify their stance using Scripture. Here's a representative example of how progressive Christian churches approach the issue of homosexuality:

The Biblical passages that have been identified historically as ones that condemn homosexuality are found in both the Hebrew (Old Testament) and the Christian (New Testament) Scriptures. Most of the Hebrew references translate the Hebrew "kedah" into the English word "homosexual" or "sodomite." The Hebrew word, however, means "temple prostitute." Judaism, as a monotheistic religion (one God), was threatened by many competing pagan religions. Many of these religions included worship of fertility gods. Worship at these pagan temples included sex (both heterosexual and homosexual). It was those practices that the Hebrew scriptures were prohibiting.[25]

Then, referencing the New Testament Scriptures, they write,

Similarly, in the Christian scriptures, the Greek word "malakos" is translated into the English word "homosexual." Malakos referred to a Greek practice of pederasty—that is, older men having sex with boys. A unique-for-the-times hallmark of the early Christian church was that it was based on mutual, affirming love and care. So pederasty would be condemned as the abusive, coercive, power-over sexual activity it is, and clearly a violation of Jesus' command to "love one another as I have loved you."[26]

In other words, progressive Christianity claims that what God prohibited in the Old Testament was not same-sex relationships but temple prostitution. And what God prohibited in the New Testament was not same-sex relationships but pederasty.

For those unfamiliar with biblical languages and the history of interpretation, this might sound convincing. But the Bible uses such specific language that a careful study of the relevant texts makes it difficult to apply any interpretation other than a clear rejection of homosexual acts.

Historically, several passages of Scripture form the basis of Christianity's position on homosexuality, notably the story of Sodom and Gomorrah (Genesis 19:1–11), the Levitical laws condemning same-sex relationships (Leviticus 18:22; 20:13), two words in two New

Testament lists of sins (1 Corinthians 6:9–10; 1 Timothy 1:10), and Paul's letter to the church at Rome (Romans 1:26–27).

I strongly encourage you to study these passages for yourself. However, I'd like to make a general observation here. Progressive Christians, in keeping with their reliance on postmodern thought, make an argument from *culture* rather than *creation*. They suggest that scriptural prohibitions on homosexuality were addressing some sort of cultural issue and should not be normative for all people throughout all time. Furthermore, their emphasis on today's cultural preferences leads them to explain away, relativize, and minimize what should be obvious: whenever the writers of both the Old and New Testaments addressed same-sex relationships, they rejected such behavior as out of alignment with God's standards and intent for human sexuality.

People will go to great lengths to justify sinful behavior rather than conform their lives to the biblical standard of holiness. That's a temptation for all of us, but it's vital that we remain vigilant and foster an attitude of humble openness to the instruction of Scripture.

Progressive Christians are also in error regarding their position on a woman's choice to terminate a pregnancy. A woman should have the right to do what she wants to do with *her own body*. The problem is that when a woman makes a decision to have an abortion, she's making a decision for *someone else's body*; namely, the body of her unborn child. That may seem like an oversimplification to some, but no matter how long I study this issue, it always boils down to that simple insight. A human being should be treated with respect and care regardless of where it's located or how small it is. Yes, pregnancy and childbirth are incredible sacrifices and extraordinary challenges for every woman who becomes a mother, but that doesn't negate the baby's right to life.

We can look for support not only to scriptures such as Psalm 139, Jeremiah 1:5, and Luke 1:41, which emphasize the value and dignity of the unborn, but also to science and medical research, which highlights the fact that even the tiniest embryo is a living creature, a human being deserving of care, respect, and protection: "Ultrasound technology has improved and evolved exponentially since the beginning. Now, life in the womb is detectable as early as 8 to 12 days post-conception. Additionally, evidence of preborn life can now be viewed through 2D, 3D and 4D ultrasounds."[27]

5. A Biblical Response to Rejection of the Atonement

I mentioned earlier that the most dangerous tendency of progressive Christianity is their rejection of the atoning work of Jesus on the cross. This is the ultimate perversion of the gospel. How do progressive Christians arrive at the idea that Jesus died not for our sins but only as an expression of sacrificial love?

It all starts with rejecting the idea of original sin and the biblical account of the fall. According to this historic Christian doctrine, all humans are born into sin because of Adam's rejection of God's law in the garden of Eden. We inherit a sin nature that separates us from God, meaning that we're born into this world needing atonement. But progressive Christianity parts ways with Christian orthodoxy:

> The story of Adam and Eve partaking of the forbidden fruit in the Garden of Eden was never intended to be read as an historical account. It is a beautifully crafted metaphorical narrative of creation and how human kind evolved into a self-conscious awareness of the reality of good and evil. The Bible never refers to Adam's disobedience as a Fall. Again, it is a story; it is not history. . . . Therefore, there could not have been a Fall because there was nothing to fall from. Jesus did not come

to rescue fallen sinners from a fall that never happened. Again, there was never any perfection from which to be corrupted.[28]

If there is no original sin, there is no need for an atonement. The article I just quoted goes on to say that God would have to be some kind of "monster God" to inflict suffering and death on "an innocent Jesus." The author rejects the historic understanding that Jesus gave His life for us, bearing the penalty that we sinful humans deserved. That erroneous line of thought leads to this stunningly questionable conclusion: "While salvation is alluded to in the gospel stories, it was never a major emphasis for Jesus or for the gospel writers. Rather than talk about salvation, Christianity should stress the importance of living lives of greater wholeness and ongoing personal transformation."[29]

To suggest that salvation was not a major emphasis for Jesus or the gospel writers is a huge stretch. But even if that were true, other New Testament writers certainly focused on salvation, which showcases once again the cherry-picking tendencies of progressive Christianity.

What does the Bible actually say about these matters of original sin, atonement, and salvation? Consider these verses regarding original sin: "Indeed, I was guilty when I was born; I was sinful when my mother conceived me" (Psalm 51:5) and "Just as sin entered the world through one man, and death through sin, in this way death spread to all people, because all sinned" (Romans 5:12).

As cute and precious as little babies are, the Bible makes it clear that every human inherits a sin nature from birth. Progressive Christians claim that Christ did not die for our sins. But this is a blatant rejection of what the Scriptures explicitly teach.

The next day John saw Jesus coming toward him and said, "Look, the Lamb of God, who takes away the sin of the world!"

—JOHN 1:29

For I passed on to you as most important what I also received: that Christ died for our sins according to the Scriptures.

—1 CORINTHIANS 15:3

He himself is the atoning sacrifice for our sins, and not only for ours, but also for those of the whole world.

—1 JOHN 2:2

You know that he was revealed so that he might take away sins, and there is no sin in him.

—1 JOHN 3:5

My friends, by now I hope you understand why it is so critical to have a solid understanding of the Bible and a strong theological foundation. A strong foundation will undergird and protect you from a plethora of false teachings designed to lead you astray.

A HEALTHY BALANCE

So what should our position be when it comes to this collection of beliefs and attitudes that characterize progressive Christianity? To summarize, progressive Christianity diverts from historical, biblical Christianity to such an extent that it's fair to question whether it can even be called Christian. Any individual or group goes against historical Christianity and the witness of Scripture if they promote the following beliefs:

- They claim Jesus isn't the divine Son of God, only a good moral example we should emulate.
- They promote an inclusive gospel in which other religions are viewed as equally valid paths to salvation.

- They seek to undermine the authority and inspiration of God's Word.
- They try to water down God's view of moral issues, thus conforming the Bible to culture or their own personal preferences.
- They deny the atoning work of Jesus Christ.

Those are all serious problems with progressive Christianity that should be vigorously guarded against. But on the other hand, let's not forget these biblical reminders:

- We should express genuine love toward people of all groups. This love doesn't mean blatant acceptance or affirmation of every behavior, decision, and lifestyle. It means treating every individual with dignity and respect as an image-bearer of God.
- We shouldn't hate, bash, or express bigotry toward those in the LGBTQ+ community, but we should stand firm on what the Bible says about such issues.
- We shouldn't be afraid to affirm Emergent or progressive critiques of modernism. Be bold in your convictions, but don't forget to remain humble and teachable, recognizing that we're all finite. And in our zeal for doctrinal correctness, may we never forget the importance of compassion and justice. While the church should discipline those living in willful sin and prohibit them from serving until they repent, we should always seek healing and restoring as we speak the truth in love.

Progressive Christianity is a powerful and alluring movement, and while I've focused primarily on its most egregious errors, there are plenty of subtle ways it misleads even well-meaning, biblically based evangelical churches. Stay alert, remain in prayer, and keep reading your Bible!

SIX

CAN I LOSE MY SALVATION?

After all of his negative experiences, Jarren was more than ready to take a break from church for a while. But he wasn't ready to take a break from his faith. He'd been saved long enough that giving up on Christianity didn't even feel like an option. He believed in Jesus and loved reading Scripture. It was just the whole church side of things that wasn't working out. So he began a personal reset, free from all the confusing messages encountered in every church he'd tried.

But not having a church community came with its own set of challenges. Jarren started falling back into old sinful patterns. Before he became a believer, he had been addicted to pornography, and the struggle had never disappeared. But for all the problems he faced in the church, Jarren almost always found strength in communities of like-minded believers who encouraged him to pursue Christlikeness in every area of life.

Now, because he was so discouraged and detached from community, the temptation to watch pornography and continue engaging in sexual sin with his girlfriend surfaced with a newly intense vengeance. He quickly sank back into the familiar addictive patterns. The disillusionment with church was now so strong that he began to question everything he had experienced.

Is my salvation real? Am I really a Christian? Wasn't I supposed to be set free from this debilitating addiction to pornography? Why haven't I been delivered from these sexual desires? Why don't I have the power to overcome them?

Jarren was at his wits' end and didn't know where else to turn for help. So he reached out to his friend Todd, who had been saved for a long time and knew about his battle with lust. They met for lunch and spent a few minutes catching up before Jarren mentally gathered his strength to bring up a more difficult topic. "The reason I called is that I've been struggling with pornography again."

Todd leaned forward, giving Jarren his complete focus. "When you say 'struggling,' what do you mean?"

"I've been watching it pretty much every night, and even a couple of times during the day," Jarren managed to admit, his mouth so dry that the words were barely audible.

"Hmm, that's not good, man," Todd said. "That was me about a year ago, and I realized I had lost my salvation. Do you think you may have lost yours?"

Jarren didn't know what to expect from Todd, but *this* came totally out of left field. "What do you mean, I might have lost my salvation?"

"I mean the Bible says that those who are truly saved won't continue in willful sin. The fact that you are continuing in blatant, willful sin may mean that you are no longer saved."

Jarren felt his anxiety level rising and he tried to take deep breaths. "Well, how would I know if I'm still saved? Is there a certain number of sins you can commit before losing your salvation or something? What if I surpassed that number a while back and didn't even know it?"

"I'm not sure. I just know you can lose it. I've lost mine a few times and had to get it back through a lot of prayer and repentance. Many people have lost their salvation, but some never seem to get it back. The key to knowing you're saved is living in victory over sin. You'll slip up from time to time, but you shouldn't be having the same struggles you had before you were a Christian. If you are, that's a pretty clear indication you're no longer saved. I'll be praying for you, bro! And know that I'm always here for you if you ever want to talk or pray about it. I hope you can get saved again."

Jarren's stomach dropped and his anxiety gave way to outright fear, with a big dose of shock and confusion. His mind raced with questions. *Have I lost my salvation? If I did, exactly how and when did it happen? How can I get it back and make sure I don't lose it again? How will I know if I've lost it the next time? How perfect do I need to be to stay saved? Isn't every sin willful to some degree? How do I know if I'm continuing to live in willful sin?*

Despite his devastation at the thought of having lost his salvation, Jarren was determined to pour himself into fighting his sin. If he could gain victory over it, he could put his doubts about his salvation to rest. But no matter how hard he tried and no matter how many victories he won, if he was being honest with himself, he wasn't living in *complete* victory over sin. If it wasn't pornography, it was sex with his girlfriend. If it wasn't that, it was something else.

A couple of months after his conversation with Todd, Jarren was completely exhausted and defeated. *My relationship with God is over*, he concluded one night. He wasn't exactly sure how and when it happened, and he had no idea how to get it back again—or even if recovering it was possible.

YOU DON'T NEED TO LIVE IN FEAR

Jarren's fear and anxiety about losing his salvation is far too common in the body of Christ. Many Christians are being misled by the lie that somehow they may have lost their salvation—or might lose it if they aren't careful. They live in the constant grip of fear that their sins will disqualify them from being a Christian. Some churches even teach that it's not

> Many live in the constant grip of fear that their sins will disqualify them from being a Christian.

really possible for a Christian to know for sure that they are saved. The good news is that God *does* want us to have assurance of our salvation, and the Bible says as much: "I have written these things to you who believe in the name of the Son of God so that you may know that you have eternal life" (1 John 5:13).

The lie that we can lose our salvation or can never know whether we're truly saved is a perversion of the true gospel, and it hinders believers from living in and embracing the freedom, peace, and joy the gospel promises.

In the pages ahead we're going to look at some important biblically supported doctrines and teachings that can set every Christian free from the fear that salvation is fragile, fleeting, or uncertain. Perhaps the most important doctrine is eternal security. Sometimes referred to as "once saved, always saved," eternal security is the theological belief that once a person places genuine faith in Jesus Christ, their salvation is eternally secure. In other words, they no longer have to fear going to hell. It is impossible for this person to lose or even forfeit their salvation.

I admit that's a very bold statement. So it's essential to support it with a strong biblical foundation that demonstrates why the opposing view doesn't stack up. Before we dig into the doctrine of eternal security, let's examine how and why it's so dangerous for a Christian to deny this doctrine of eternal security.

THE CONSEQUENCES OF DENYING ETERNAL SECURITY

Understanding this doctrine of eternal security is not just some theological exercise to make you sound intelligent. The way you view your salvation has ramifications for how you relate to God and live your daily life as a Christian. If you believe your salvation is on shaky ground, you will relate to God on the basis of fear rather than faith. Everything you do for Him will be motivated by fear rather than love.

Denying this doctrine will inevitably set up a legalistic relationship between you and God. Legalism demands that you perfectly adhere to a set of rules to secure or keep your salvation. It also suggests that God's love for you and His acceptance of you fluctuates depending on your behavior.

Instead of experiencing the peace and joy that come from knowing your salvation is secure, you will live in a constant state of uncertainty, wondering day after day if you've done enough to keep from losing your salvation. That uncertainty might make you try to get saved and baptized again and again just to make sure you're going to heaven. My friend, God doesn't want that for you. He wants you to be free. He wants you to enjoy the peace and freedom that come from knowing what your Savior did for you on the cross.

BIBLICAL PILLARS OF ETERNAL SECURITY

I liken eternal security to a house with eight pillars. Each of these pillars is essential for this house to stand. I hope this chapter provides you with such overwhelming biblical evidence for the security of your salvation that you'll never doubt it again.

Pillar #1: Perseverance

This first pillar is that of *perseverance*, or the perseverance of the saints. This doctrine states that those who are truly born again will be empowered by the Spirit to continue to believe until the day they die. We don't persevere in our own strength. We persevere because the Spirit of God, who lives within us, empowers us to do so. Several scriptures support this teaching: "Therefore, my dear friends, just as you have always obeyed, so now, not only in my presence but even more in my absence, work out your own salvation with fear and trembling. For

> We persevere because the Spirit of God, who lives within us, empowers us to do so.

it is God who is working in you both to will and to work according to his good purpose" (Philippians 2:12–13).

Notice that we're encouraged to work *out* our salvation, not work *for* it. There is a huge difference between the words *out* and *for*! Working *for* our salvation would imply that we must do something to earn it or complete it.

Working *out* our salvation implies that we're already saved, and we are simply trying to grow in our faith and sanctification. To echo Charles Spurgeon, we are "working *out*" what has already been "worked *in*."[1]

As Spurgeon pointed out, God has already worked His salvation in us, and we are simply working it out in our daily lives. This raises some good questions you may be wondering about: Couldn't a Christian simply walk away from the faith and give up on the entire thing? Can't *they* decide at any point that they no longer want to be a Christian? In other words, can a Christian renounce or forfeit their own faith and thus not persevere?

Before we answer that, it's critical that we establish one very important truth: There is a difference between *genuine* Christians and *professing* Christians. Some *profess* to be Christians but are not. They seem like Christians, at least on the surface. They attend church like Christians. They give money like Christians. They talk like Christians. They may even listen to Christian music! But none of these things mean they are actually Christians. Jesus warned about this:

> "Not everyone who says to me, 'Lord, Lord,' will enter the kingdom of heaven, but only the one who does the will of my Father in heaven.

On that day many will say to me, 'Lord, Lord, didn't we prophesy in your name, drive out demons in your name, and do many miracles in your name?' Then I will announce to them, 'I never knew you. Depart from me, you lawbreakers!'"

—MATTHEW 7:21–23

There are a few important details to highlight in this passage. First, the people were *saying* the right things. But Jesus said that many who say, "Lord, Lord," will not enter the kingdom of heaven. Second, they were *doing* what appeared to be the right things. They were involved in religious activities that most people would attribute to Christians. Third, based on what they said to Jesus on the Day of Judgment, these people seemed to be depending on these religious activities to get them into heaven. But religious activities don't save us. We're saved by grace alone through a genuine belief in the finished work of Jesus Christ on the cross. Fourth and finally, focus on four very important words: *I never knew you.* Jesus did *not* say, "I don't know you anymore." That would have implied a previous relationship that had been lost. The fact that He said I *never* knew you reveals that there was never a relationship to begin with.

So *professing* Christians can turn away from the faith because their faith wasn't genuine in the first place. This is called apostasy. Genuine Christians cannot apostatize. In other words, genuine Christians will not *totally* and *finally* turn away from the faith. Let's define these two words. *Totally* means that genuine Christians may struggle in some aspects of their faith, but they won't renounce Christianity entirely. *Finally* means that it is quite possible and common, for that matter, for genuine Christians to experience a *temporary* lapse in their faith, but they will return at some point.

Another consideration that relates to the question of whether a genuine Christian can renounce their faith involves how Jesus described genuine salvation. In John 3, Jesus said that we must be "born again." Let's analyze this concept. When a person is born physically, is there anything they can do to undo that fact? You may say, "Well, they can commit suicide." While that's true, it doesn't negate the fact that they were born first. Does that make sense? Taking one's life doesn't erase the fact that they were born. In the same way, once a person is born again, there is nothing they can do to undo their spiritual birth. Just as babies have nothing to do with their physical birth, a person who is born again has nothing to do with their spiritual rebirth.

Another scripture that strongly supports the distinction between genuine Christians and those who are merely professing Christians is 1 John 2:19: "They went out from us, but they did not belong to us; for if they had belonged to us, they would have remained with us. However, they went out so that it might be made clear that none of them belongs to us."

To summarize, there can only be three possible explanations for leaving the faith. The first possibility is that they were never saved to begin with. They professed to be but were never truly converted. The second possibility is that they remain saved but will be severely disciplined by their Father (see Hebrews 12). The third possibility is that they are in an extreme but temporary state of backsliding and rebellion, but God knows they will return to Him later.

The Bible teaches that those who are truly regenerate will indeed persevere in the faith. Perseverance is not something we do to earn our salvation, but rather something God empowers us to do to keep us walking in the salvation He's already given us.

Pillar #2: Preservation

The second pillar sounds quite similar to the first, and some theologians see preservation as synonymous with perseverance. But while perseverance of the saints focuses on being empowered by the Spirit to persevere, the preservation of the saints focuses on God's power to keep us in spite of ourselves. In short, they are two sides of the same coin. They are essentially the same doctrine seen from two different perspectives. Consider the apostle Paul's words to the church in Philippi: "I am sure of this, that he who started a good work in you will carry it on to completion until the day of Christ Jesus" (Philippians 1:6).

To be fair to the text, the second-person pronoun *you* is plural here, which means that Paul was speaking to the entire church body. However, it's reasonable to apply this statement to individual believers as part of that body. Paul insisted that since God has started the work of salvation in us, He is committed to completing it. Notice that it doesn't say God will continue to work on us only as long as we avoid sin. It doesn't say that He'll keep working on us unless we choose to walk away. It says that God is committed to continue the work He began in us "until the day of Christ Jesus." There's no indication that anything we could do would change or diminish God's resolve. Another verse communicates this idea even more strongly: "Now to him who is able to protect you from stumbling and to make you stand in the presence of his glory, without blemish and with great joy" (Jude 24).

Isn't that great news? We serve a God who is able to protect us from stumbling and *make* us stand in the presence of His glory without blemish. What a promise! This means that God's power to keep us is greater than our sin or even our attempts to walk away from Him in moments of doubt or weakness!

The apostle Peter joined the chorus of confidence in God's desire and ability to hold on to each of His children: "You are being guarded by God's power through faith for a salvation that is ready to be revealed in the last time" (1 Peter 1:5).

Are you catching the pattern here? God is guarding us with *His* power. Another classic passage that communicates this is found in

John's gospel, where Jesus declared, "I give them eternal life, and they will never perish. No one will snatch them out of my hand. My Father, who has given them to me, is greater than all. No one is able to snatch them out of the Father's hand" (John 10:28–29).

It's impossible for anyone (that includes you and me, by the way) to snatch us out of Jesus' hand. And if that's not enough, we are safe in the Father's hand as well. This passage doesn't say, "No one but the person I've given eternal life will be able to snatch them out of my hand." Jesus said exactly what He meant: no one is able to snatch us out of God's hands.

Finally, Romans 8:38–39 drives this point home: "For I am persuaded that neither death nor life, nor angels nor rulers, nor things present nor things to come, nor powers, nor height nor depth, nor any other created thing will be able to separate us from the love of God that is in Christ Jesus our Lord."

Paul's list is comprehensive. *Nothing* can separate us from the love of God. The Greek term for "nothing" actually means "*nothing*"![2] This second pillar really helps us understand just how strong God's ability is to protect us, even from ourselves. God is not a God who is strong enough to save us and yet too weak to keep us saved. He's a loving Father who will do whatever He needs to do to protect us.

Pillar #3: Predestination

If you're not sure that the first two pillars are strong enough to support the doctrine of eternal security, we have six more. *Predestination* is a fancy theological word that simply means "to determine something beforehand." Before we look to Scripture for evidence of this doctrine, let's think about something logically. If God has predetermined something to happen beforehand, do we really think we have the power to override what He has determined? I'll let you wrestle with that. Romans 8:29–30 says, "For those he foreknew he also predestined to be conformed to the image of his Son, so that he would be the firstborn among many brothers and sisters. And those he predestined, he also called; and those he called, he also justified; and those he justified, he also glorified."

Notice who is responsible for doing all of this work. It's not us; it's God. *God* has predestined believers to be conformed to the image of His Son. *God* has called us. *God* has justified us. *God* has glorified us. All of these verbs in the underlying Greek text are in what's called the aorist tense. This tense communicates an action that took place sometime in the past. Think of it like a snapshot. In the divine mind, this entire process is as good as done even though we're experiencing the outworking of God's plan in real time.

The next two scriptures reveal when God predetermined our salvation. Finally, in Romans, Paul discussed how God chose Jacob over Esau even before either of them was born:

> He has saved us and called us with a holy calling, not according to our works, but according to his own purpose and grace, which was given to us in Christ Jesus before time began.
>
> —2 TIMOTHY 1:9

> He chose us in him, before the foundation of the world, to be holy and blameless in love before him.
>
> —EPHESIANS 1:4

> For though her sons had not been born yet or done anything good or bad, so that God's purpose according to election might stand—not from works but from the one who calls—she was told, The older will serve the younger. As it is written: I have loved Jacob, but I have hated Esau.
>
> —ROMANS 9:11–13

Did you catch that? Let's unpack the implications of these verses. God sovereignly chose Jacob over Esau. Why? Because He's God and He can do what He wants to do. Was Jacob perfect and deserving of God's election? Not at all. God's choice is not based on anything we have done or anything God knows we will do. It is based entirely on His own grace.

If God chose us before the foundation of the world, He knew every sin and every decision we'd make before we made them. To suggest otherwise would deny His omniscience. This means that nothing we do, say, or think in real time catches God off guard. If we believe we can lose our salvation as a result of a certain number of sins, this implies that when God saved us before the foundation of the world, He was unaware of some of the sins we'd commit. Do you see where this logic breaks down? According to these verses, if we assert that a person can lose their salvation, we must also deny God's omniscience.

> If we assert that a person can lose their salvation, we must also deny God's omniscience.

To summarize, the Bible clearly teaches the doctrine of predestination. To say that a believer can lose or forfeit their salvation not only contradicts God's omniscience but also undermines the doctrine of predestination and suggests that a mere mortal human being can undo something that God determined beforehand.

Pillar #4: Propitiation

Propitiation is another fancy theological word that is synonymous with *atonement*, which refers to the idea that God's wrath against sinners has been appeased or satisfied. How is this possible? It's possible because of the shed blood of Jesus Christ on the cross. In the Old Testament, sacrifices continually had to be made. Every animal sacrifice or offering was partial, temporary, and provisional. But in the new covenant, Jesus was the ultimate and final sacrifice. He made "one sacrifice for sins forever" and then "sat down at the right hand of God" (Hebrews 10:12), indicating that His work was complete. And so "by one offering he has perfected forever those who are sanctified" (verse 14).

If we say that someone can lose their salvation, we are essentially saying that the sacrifice Jesus made for us on the cross wasn't sufficient to cover *all* of our sins. It was only sufficient to cover some. But once we reach some unknown sin quota, His sacrifice is null and void, and we're on our own.

This lie that we can lose our salvation perverts the gospel. The gospel, or good news, is the fact that, to borrow a formula from Beau Lee, "Jesus plus nothing equals salvation."[3] As soon as we add something to that equation, it is no longer good news. It's bad news because we will never be able to work enough to earn our salvation! Far too many Christians are living by the following formula:

Jesus + My Works = My Salvation

The apostle Paul vehemently condemned this notion in these powerful words: "You are saved by grace through faith, and this is not from yourselves; it is God's gift—not from works, so that no one can boast" (Ephesians 2:8–9).

Paul emphasized in a few different ways that our salvation is a work of God and not a work we as human beings accomplish. First, he called that work "grace," which means "unmerited or unearned favor." Second, he said that our salvation is "not from yourselves," which means we are not the originators of our own salvation. It is strictly a work of God (Hebrews 12:2). Third, he says it's God's gift. A gift is not something we earn. It's given freely.

Fourth, Paul emphasized that salvation is "not from works," which means there is nothing we could do to earn it, and no one is saved because of anything they've done. I'm not saved because I resisted sin any more than the person who is currently sitting next to me on this plane (yes, I'm on a plane writing these words). Finally, he reminds us that God set all of this up "so that no one can boast." God doesn't want anyone in heaven boasting that they are there because of anything *they* were able to do. The moment we add works, we pervert the gospel and imply that what Jesus did wasn't good enough.

The Bible says that "Christ also suffered for sins once for all, the righteous for the unrighteous, that he might bring you to God. He was put to death in the flesh but made alive by the Spirit" (1 Peter 3:18). Let me emphasize that word *all*. Jesus suffered and died for *all* of our sins, not just some of them.

Those who suggest a person can lose their salvation as a result of sinning too much are never able to explain two things. First, what sins would someone have to commit to lose their salvation? Continual sexual sin? Living in a constant state of unforgiveness toward those who have offended you? It's never quite clear. Second, how does a person know they have lost their salvation? Without clarity about how salvation is lost, people live in fear that their next sin might be the tipping point. But Scripture should set our hearts and minds at peace, assuring us that Christ's once-and-for-all sacrifice covers all sins, making fears about accidently losing our salvation completely unfounded.

I'm reminded of the words of one of my favorite hymns, "It Is Well with My Soul," which says,

> *My sin—O the bliss of this glorious thought* [a thought]
> *My sin, not in part, but the whole* [every bit, all of it]
> *Is nailed to the cross, and I bear it no more* [yes!]
> *Praise the Lord, praise the Lord, O my soul!*[4]

The only way it can truly be well with your soul is if you know that your sins are completely forgiven.

Pillar #5: Permanence

The New Testament writers describe our salvation as *permanent*. Jesus Himself said, "Truly I tell you, anyone who hears my word and believes him who sent me has eternal life and will not come under judgment but has passed from death to life" (John 5:24).

The Greek word translated "eternal" in this passage doesn't have a secret meaning. *Eternal* means exactly what you think it means: forever![5] Jesus didn't say that if we believe in Him, we'll have life until we sin or forfeit our salvation. He said that we immediately inherit *eternal life*. He also declared that when we believe, we have "passed from death to life." No other conditions have been added to this verse.

The most famous verse in the entire Bible says, "For God loved the world in this way: He gave his one and only Son, so that everyone who believes in him will not perish but have eternal life" (John 3:16). The bottom line is that either our salvation is eternal or it's not. And if it's eternal, that means that it cannot also be temporary.

Pillar #6: Promises

God has made certain promises to believers. For us to lose our salvation would mean that God has reneged on His promises. For instance, Ephesians 1:13 says, "In him you also were sealed with the promised Holy Spirit when you heard the word of truth, the gospel of your salvation, and when you believed."

Notice that the sealing doesn't take place sometime in the future. It happens right when we get saved. It happens when we hear the word of truth and believe! The next verse says, "The Holy Spirit is the down payment of our inheritance, until the redemption of the possession, to the praise of his glory" (verse 14).

I love the imagery Paul uses here of a down payment. When we put money down on a home, we are making a promise to take full possession of that home at some point in the future. The down payment is our way of entering into a contract. Well, God has entered into something much stronger than a contract with us. He's entered into a covenant with His children, a unilateral covenant He cannot break. The down payment is the Holy Spirit. For God to remove His Holy Spirit from us would be like breaking a contract on a home. This is not consistent with His nature or character.

Hebrews 8:6 says, "Jesus has now obtained a superior ministry, and to that degree he is the mediator of a better covenant, which has been established on better promises." This verse emphasizes that the covenant we're under is a *better* covenant than God's covenant with the people of Israel under the law of Moses, because it's established on *better* promises. Now here is the clincher. This new covenant is discussed in detail in Jeremiah 32. To be fair to the text, this new covenant was described as a covenant that God would enter into with the nation of Israel. However, by extension, the church benefits from it as well. Through the prophet Jeremiah, God described the nature of this covenant: "I will make a permanent covenant with them: I will never turn away from doing good to them, and I will put fear of me in their hearts so they will never again turn away from me" (Jeremiah 32:40).

This is rich theological language. The new covenant is *permanent*. Our salvation is based on a promise from God, and God cannot break that promise. It is secure!

Pillar #7: Prayers

The Bible teaches that as part of Jesus' high priestly ministry, He sits at the right hand of the Father right now making intercession for the saints: "Therefore, he is able to save completely those who come to God through him, since he always lives to intercede for them" (Hebrews 7:25).

Did you catch the *reason* why Jesus is able to "save completely those who come to God through him"? Because He is constantly interceding for us. Jesus, the Son of God, is interceding with the Father on our behalf. We could not be any more secure than that. Isn't it a comfort to know that Jesus is constantly interceding for us with the Father? The beautiful thing is that Jesus understands what we're going through. "Therefore, since we have a great high priest who has passed through the

> Isn't it a comfort to know that Jesus is constantly interceding for us with the Father?

heavens—Jesus the Son of God—let us hold fast to our confession. For we do not have a high priest who is unable to sympathize with our weaknesses, but one who has been tempted in every way as we are, yet without sin" (Hebrews 4:14–15).

Because Jesus has been through everything we've been through and will go through, He is most qualified to intercede with God the Father on our behalf.

Pillar #8: Pictures

God gives us some beautiful pictures of salvation in the book of Ephesians that communicate the certainty of our salvation. Let's explore these powerful images.

The Picture of Adoption

The Bible says that when we were saved, we were adopted into God's family: "He predestined us to be adopted as sons through Jesus Christ for himself, according to the good pleasure of his will" (Ephesians 1:5).

Think about this for a moment. When a parent adopts a child, that child will forever belong to the parent. There is no way that child can undo the fact they have been adopted. They belong to those parents forever. In the same way, our adoption into God's family is final, and there is nothing we can do to change it.

The Picture of a Slave

In Ephesians 1:7 we read, "In him we have redemption through his blood . . ." The Greek word translated "redemption" essentially means "buying back" a slave or captive (i.e., "making free" by payment of a ransom).[6] The picture Paul painted here is that of a slave. We were slaves to sin. We had no power to break the yoke of sin in our lives. But Jesus loved us enough that He paid the price to set us free from sin's bondage, never to return to slavery. Do you think God would purchase a slave and then allow that slave to return to bondage? Here's a better question: If someone was truly enslaved and then was set free, would they want to return to being a slave? The answer is no in both instances.

The Picture of a Criminal

Ephesians 1:7 also tells us that in Christ "we have . . . the forgiveness of our trespasses, according to the riches of his grace." The Greek word for "forgiveness" means "the act of freeing from an obligation, guilt, or punishment, pardon, cancellation."[7] When Jesus saved us, He canceled our debt of sin. The picture in Ephesians is of one who knows they are guilty as they stand before a judge. The judge has every right to sentence them to life in prison, and the convicted criminal knows it. But instead, someone else pays their debt and serves the life sentence in their place.

If this person has been set free from the penalty of life in prison, would they want to return to being a convicted criminal? Or would they want to spend their lives expressing their joy and appreciation to the one who paid the price for their freedom? The pictures God paints concerning our salvation suggest that our salvation is secure. There are verses sprinkled throughout the New Testament that, on the surface, sound as if a believer can lose or forfeit their salvation. A detailed discussion of these passages is outside the scope of this book, but if you carefully study them in their proper context, you'll discover these verses don't actually mean that a Christian can lose their salvation. The biblical evidence suggesting that a believer's salvation is secure is overwhelming.

DOES ETERNAL SECURITY TEACH LICENSE?

The most compelling criticism of eternal security comes from those who claim it indirectly gives people a license to sin. According to these critics, the doctrine essentially says, "Go ahead and sin. After all, you'll still be saved, so don't worry about holiness!" The Bible doesn't teach this at all. As a matter of fact, it teaches the opposite: "The law came along to multiply the trespass. But where sin multiplied, grace multiplied even more" (Romans 5:20).

At first glance, it may appear that Paul was giving people a license to sin. If God's forgiving grace is always greater than our sin, why bother expending too much energy on avoiding sin? While grace's complete power over sin is undeniable, Paul anticipated the misconception and immediately set the record straight: "What should we say then? Should we continue in sin so that grace may multiply? Absolutely not! How can we who died to sin still live in it?" (Romans 6:1–2).

In Paul's mind, looking at grace as an excuse to sin is inconceivable. It's inconceivable to think that a person who experiences God's grace would *want* to take advantage of it. Such an attitude is not what the new nature leads believers toward. Here's where the new nature *does* lead: "And do not offer any parts of it to sin as weapons for unrighteousness. But as those who are alive from the dead, offer yourselves to God, and all the parts of yourselves to God as weapons for righteousness" (Romans 6:13). The new nature prompts believers to offer their entire being to God as "weapons for righteousness," not for unrighteousness.

A HEALTHY BALANCE

How do we harmonize eternal security with our ongoing struggle with sin? What does it look like for a believer to live with confidence and peace in light of God's grace while also pursuing holiness with a sincere heart?

First, we rest in the assurance of our salvation. This assurance is itself a gift God wants us to have. This doesn't mean we won't continue to struggle with sin. Even the great apostle Paul struggled with sin, describing it as a war in Romans 7:14–25.

Elsewhere Paul even referred to himself as the chief of sinners: "This is a faithful saying and worthy of all acceptance, that Christ Jesus came into the world to save sinners, of whom I am chief" (1 Timothy 1:15 NKJV). Did you notice that Paul used the present tense? He didn't say he *was* the chief; he said "of whom I *am* chief."

Second, when we experience true conversion, we're no longer happy to continue in our old sinful lifestyles. In our struggle against sin, we don't want to take advantage of God's grace. That abundant grace is not a license to sin but an insurance policy. We're grateful we have it in case we need it, but we would prefer not to use it if we don't have to. Wouldn't it be weird for someone to *enjoy* using their insurance policy again and again?

If you feel yourself treating sin casually, remember that the grace that won your forgiveness wasn't cheap; it was purchased at an unfathomable cost. The tighter you hold to grace, the less attractive sin will be and the more confidence you will have in the salvation God has given you. Make a habit of thanking God for the assurance of your salvation and embrace the reality that He chose you before the foundation of the world.

SEVEN

CAN I BE SAVED AND NOT BE A DISCIPLE?

onvinced that he had lost his salvation, Jarren wasn't eager to start attending church again. He knew that whenever he heard a sermon about sin, it would just increase his fear that he wasn't saved and leave him feeling more defeated than ever. But no matter how hard he tried, he just couldn't win complete and total victory over his sin, especially his addiction to pornography.

For several months Jarren went through a cycle of getting saved again (repeating some version of the sinner's prayer), followed by a brief experience of joy, freedom, and excitement before he would lapse into sexual sin or some other sin and fall back into despair. The cycle was exhausting and disheartening. *How can I say I'm a Christian while continuing to do this and offend God?* he asked himself over and over. But as the weeks passed, Jarren felt his spiritual fire starting to burn out. He began to grow cold toward prayer and Scripture and stopped thinking about attending a church.

One day Jarren was walking through the mall when a friend from the church he'd attended the previous year called out his name. "Hey, Jarren, long time no see. What have you been up to?"

Jarren was glad to see a friendly face but immediately felt awkward about the inevitable church conversation. "Hey, good to see you," he said. "Sorry I haven't been to church in a while. I needed a break."

"No worries, bro. The same thing happened to me."

"Really?" Jarren asked.

"Yep, just got burned out trying to be perfect and realized I couldn't be. Now I attend another church and it's totally different. It's nothing like our old church."

In spite of himself, Jarren was once again intrigued at the thought of a different type of church—perhaps the one that would have the answers he'd sought for so long. "For real? Tell me about it."

"It's called Grace Abounds Fellowship. Essentially they've taught me that we no longer have to confess our sins to God or even repent because we've already been forgiven for all of our past, present, and future sins. Think about it. If this is true, what is the real point of confessing sins to God that He already knows about and has already forgiven us for? It's actually kind of offensive to God to ask Him for forgiveness for something He's already forgiven us for. It's like we don't really believe He's forgiven us."

Jarren mentally reviewed the passages he was familiar with about God's grace and forgiveness, and on a cursory level his friend's assertions seemed to check out. "You know, that's a good point, but I never thought of it that way," he said.

"Yeah, it makes total sense. I'm not sure how I missed it for so long! I can tell you it's worked wonders for my spiritual life. It's like a load has been lifted off me. I can just focus on living for God without constantly being bogged down by my sin. I don't even think about my sin anymore. I mean, I'm aware of it, but I don't give it a passing thought beyond that. My emotional and spiritual state has never been better."

By the time they parted ways that afternoon, Jarren had agreed to check out Grace Abounds Fellowship. Maybe a bigger focus on grace was the missing ingredient all along. And sure enough, as soon as Jarren began attending he felt a sense of freedom. He had been carrying the weight of his porn addiction for a year now. Coming to the realization that he didn't have to confess it or repent of it anymore made him feel free in a way he hadn't for many months. He was even managing to let go of the fear that he was no longer saved. The pastor's focus in every sermon was on the completeness and finality of grace and forgiveness.

Jarren continued to watch pornography from time to time, but he kept his focus on the reality that he was already forgiven. Well, if he was being truly honest, watching pornography wasn't just happening from time to time. If anything, he was watching more than ever.

But he finally felt comfortable at church. He was encouraged by the warm, inviting community. He loved the weekly reminders of God's grace. And while he wasn't praying or reading his Bible like he had when he first became a Christian, Jarren figured that was just part of the faith journey. The intense love for Jesus, the joy of the gospel, and a passion for studying the Word and spending time in prayer had been great while they lasted, but they probably weren't sustainable over the long term. Besides, he'd faced some serious ups and downs, including what now seemed like needlessly difficult battles with guilt, fear, and confusion. Maybe he'd finally found the right balance and the right church.

FALSE ASSURANCE

In the previous chapter we discussed the beautiful doctrine of eternal security, the assurance of our salvation as a gift that God gives to every believer. He wants to give us peace and joy as we rest in the finished work of Jesus Christ on the cross. But as dangerous as it is for genuine believers to question their salvation, it's equally if not more dangerous for professing Christians to be assured of their salvation when they *aren't* really saved.

The danger is assuming that a person is saved just because they prayed a prayer and got baptized—even if their lives display very little, if any, Christian fruit years later. In his book *The Cost of Discipleship*, theologian Dietrich Bonhoeffer described this as "cheap grace."[1] He challenged the idea that you can receive eternal life simply by reciting a quick prayer. Genuine believers are secure in their salvation, but there is a danger for those who profess to be saved but aren't. The Bible is clear that on judgment day many will be surprised: "On that day many will say to me, 'Lord, Lord, didn't we prophesy in your name, drive out demons in your name, and do many miracles in your name?' Then I will announce to them, 'I never knew you. Depart from me, you law-breakers!'" (Matthew 7:22–23).

It's all too common for people to be *professing* Christians but not *genuine* Christians. To be clear, the false teaching I am referring to in this chapter is the idea that you can be a Christian while showing few, if any, signs of spiritual growth. This is a message that *must* be discussed, and I pray that you hear my heart on this. Some of the other false teachings we have discussed in this book will not affect where you spend eternity. You can speak in tongues or not, and false beliefs about that gift might cause you harm without affecting your salvation. You can be led astray by a false prophet. You can pray and trust God for a healing or a financial breakthrough He's never promised you. You can try to speak things into existence all day long. You can do all of these things and still be saved. You might be frustrated or disillusioned or confused but still have a genuine, saving faith.

> It's all too common for people to be *professing* Christians but not *genuine* Christians.

But what we discuss in this chapter could determine your eternal destiny. I don't say that lightly. We'll define what cheap grace is and how and why it's so dangerous to the body of Christ. Then we'll look at what hinders some professing Christians from progressing toward genuine Christianity. We'll also examine four different categories that characterize people on their spiritual journeys. Finally, we'll identify what God desires to see in the life of a true, authentic believer.

WHAT IS CHEAP GRACE?

What exactly is cheap grace? As you read this quote from Dietrich Bonhoeffer, ask yourself if this is what we see promoted in our culture and our churches today:

> Cheap grace is the deadly enemy of our church. . . . [It is] grace without price; grace without cost! . . . Cheap grace means grace as a doctrine . . . an intellectual assent. . . . Cheap grace means the justification of sin without the justification of the sinner. . . . Cheap grace is the grace we bestow on ourselves. Cheap grace is the preaching of forgiveness without requiring repentance, baptism without church discipline, Communion without confession, absolution without personal confession. Cheap grace is grace without discipleship, grace without the cross, grace without Jesus Christ, living and incarnate. . . .
>
> Costly grace is the gospel which must be sought again and again. . . . Such grace is costly because it calls us to follow, and it is grace because it calls us to follow Jesus Christ. It is costly because it costs a man his life, and it is grace because it gives a man the only true life. It is costly because it condemns sin, and grace because it justifies the sinner. Above all, it is costly because it cost God the life of his Son: "ye were bought at a price," and what has cost God much cannot be cheap for us. Above all, it is grace because God did not reckon his Son too dear a price to pay for our life, but delivered him up for us. Costly grace is the Incarnation of God.[2]

Wow! Each of those words should resonate within the life of every true believer. Bonhoeffer noticed back in 1937 that people were abusing the doctrine of grace. They were living as carnal Christians (which we'll discuss later). They were buying into the lie that salvation is nothing more than cheap fire insurance to protect us from the flames of hell. Robbie Castleman described it like this: "Cheap grace sells us a comfortable Jesus to whom we sing affectionate valentines. Cheap grace substitutes the fear of the Lord for a fear of the world. . . . Salvation is a free gift of God's grace earned by the work of Jesus Christ alone. And this free gift will cost you everything."[3]

Many professing Christians want the benefits of Christianity (such as salvation, prayer, provision, and protection) without any of the sacrifices. They treat God like a spare tire, considering Him only when they need something. Their lives are characterized by worldly living and whatever makes them happy, with very little regard for the things of God. All the while, these people claim the name Christian.

I'm here to tell you that it's possible to be a churchgoer and apparently a decent person—and be headed straight to hell. Sorry to put it so bluntly, but someone has to. You may be reading this book right now, and this is *exactly* what you need to hear.

To be clear, I'm not suggesting that something other than faith is required to earn or maintain your salvation. Ephesians 2:8–9 and many other scriptures make it abundantly clear that we are saved only by placing our faith in Jesus Christ. No amount of works can save us or keep us saved. But some erroneously conclude that because they expressed faith in God, filled out a decision card, walked down the aisle, recited a prayer, and attended a new members' class, they must be saved. All of that is a great start. But sadly, this is where many people end.

HOW DOES THIS HAPPEN?

Why are there so many professing Christians who aren't genuinely walking with God? How exactly did we get to this point? I suggest that there are three ways this can happen.

The Church Has No Discipleship Plan

I may get in trouble for this, but I'm willing to take that risk. Some of the responsibility for why we have so many professing Christians lies with churches, which have largely failed in their most important mission: making disciples. "Jesus came near and said to them, 'All authority has been given to me in heaven and on earth. Go, therefore, and make disciples of all nations, baptizing them in the name of the Father and of the Son and of the Holy Spirit, teaching them to observe everything I have commanded you. And remember, I am with you always, to the end of the age'" (Matthew 28:18–20).

Jesus didn't say we should make professing Christians (though making a profession of faith is a vital step). He didn't say that we should build a bunch of church buildings (though it's great to have places to gather). He said to make disciples. People need to be discipled so they can make other disciples, but many churches don't have a specific discipleship strategy. They have a strategy to help new members get oriented to their church. They have a strategy for plugging people into small groups. They have a strategy for getting people to volunteer their time and serve in various ministries. But all those strategies and activities may not lead to real discipleship.

The result? We have a generation of people who have been deceived into thinking they are Christians because they walked down the aisle, said a prayer, attend church, and give money—but their lives exhibit very little fruit. And no wonder. They have never been challenged to do so! Every church should have a clear strategy for how to take someone *professing* Christ to being a fully devoted *follower* of Christ.

People Are Confused About What a Disciple Is

That brings us to a second reason why so many profess to be Christians but are not actually walking with Jesus: in many cases, no one has ever made clear to them what Jesus desires from those who follow Him. What exactly is a disciple? Let's look at what Jesus Himself said about those who want to follow Him from Luke 14. As we walk through these verses, ask yourself whether messages like this are being promoted in your church and in the fellowship of believers with whom you spend your time. By the way, this text is one of the central inspirations of Bonhoeffer's work.

"Now great crowds were traveling with him. So he turned and said to them, 'If anyone comes to me . . .'" (Luke 14:25–26). Notice the scope of Jesus' message. He was setting up a universal standard for anyone who wanted to follow Him. I emphasize this because it's easy for many Christians to think that certain standards apply only to church leaders, pastors, missionaries, or seminary students. But Jesus didn't make that distinction. What He was about to say applies to *everyone* who claims to be a disciple of Christ. Let's examine the primary features of a disciple according to Jesus:

> "If anyone comes to me and does not hate his own father and mother, wife and children, brothers and sisters—yes, and even his own life—he cannot be my disciple. Whoever does not bear his own cross and come after me cannot be my disciple. For which of you, wanting to build a tower, doesn't first sit down and calculate the cost to see if he has enough to complete it? Otherwise, after he has laid the foundation and cannot finish it, all the onlookers will begin to ridicule him, saying, 'This man started to build and wasn't able to finish.'" (Luke 14:26–30)

Allegiance Over Apathy

If anyone does not hate his own father and mother . . . (verse 26). This is a surprising passage, but it boils down to priorities and allegiance. Essentially, Jesus was saying that we should have no greater allegiance than to Him. To make it abundantly clear, He said that the gap between our allegiance to our families and to Him ought to be so wide that compared to how deeply devoted we are to Him, it should appear as though we hate others, even those we love the most. Of course we're not supposed to actually hate our families; Jesus was using hyperbole and contrast to emphasize the absolute priority of our allegiance to Him. When people profess to be Christians, we ought to ask them if they are prepared to pledge their allegiance to Christ above and beyond all other earthly relationships.

Sacrifice Over Self-Centeredness

If anyone does not hate even his own life . . . (verse 26). If we aren't ready to lay down our lives in complete surrender, we cannot be His disciples. I hope you hear what Jesus was saying. He was narrowing the road, setting His expectations for those who truly want to follow Him. He was raising the bar. Unfortunately, we lower the bar in many of our churches today. Jesus asks for full surrender, but sadly many of us give so little for He who gave so much.

> If we aren't ready to lay down our lives in complete surrender, we cannot be Jesus' disciples.

Pain Over Pleasure

Whoever does not bear his own cross . . . (verse 27). Being a disciple of Jesus involves pain. It won't be all peaches and cream. We may have to suffer. Try preaching this in your church and see how many people stick around! We may have to stay in a difficult marriage when it doesn't feel good. We may have to stay faithful to a spouse who isn't meeting our needs for an extended period of time. What we see far too often in our culture are Christians who elevate their personal happiness above the perfect will of God for their lives.

Relationship Over Religion

Whoever does not come after me . . . (verse 27). Ooh, this one is going to hurt. Jesus says that we not only need to bear our own cross, but we also need to "come after" Him. In other words, Jesus is inviting us into an intimate relationship with Him that extends far beyond following a bunch of religious rules, attending church every Sunday, or giving a certain percentage of our income to a church. True followers cultivate their relationship with Jesus.

For a moment, let's set aside the deep sacrifice implied by taking up our crosses and simply ask ourselves whether we're prioritizing our relationship with Jesus. How much of our time do we devote to prayer, the study of Scripture, and the teachings of Christianity? A Barna survey revealed that almost half of evangelicals read their Bible only once a week or not at all.[4] Other studies have shown that most Christians don't even know the basic teachings and beliefs of the faith.

When I was in seminary, I had the privilege of learning under the late Dr. Howard Hendricks. His Bible Study Methods course was the first class I took at Dallas Theological Seminary. One thing I'll never forget is when he told me that for fifty years in a row he had read through the Bible cover to cover. I was so convicted because here I was, a seminary student, and up to that point I could probably count on two or three fingers how many times I had read the entire Bible. Dr. Hendricks is an example of a man who prioritized his relationship with Jesus. Even if we live in a time or place where being a disciple of Jesus doesn't involve risking life and limb, are we making it a priority to "come after" Him?

Commitment Over Convenience

Which of you doesn't calculate the cost? (verse 28). This is where Jesus challenged His listeners to truly consider if following Him was something they wanted to do. Is this a journey they wanted to embark on, a project they were willing to see through to the end? People who want to build a tower can't just jump into the endeavor. They consider the cost first, and *then* they commit. Maybe if we shared Jesus' words with people before they fill out a decision card and pray the salvation prayer, fewer of them would foreclose on their faith a year later. Notice what happens when people don't consider the cost of following Jesus.

Faithfulness Over Fickleness

After he has laid the foundation . . . (verses 29–30). Isn't this exactly what we see happening today? People have "laid the foundation" for their faith but are not able to follow through. They quit. They quit their marriages. They quit their churches. They quit their faith.

The account in Luke 14 started out with Jesus talking to large crowds. I imagine few people responding positively to His message. It is my prayer that you and I would ask ourselves whether we are part of the *crowd* or the *committed*. When Jesus called someone to follow Him, He was challenging them to a life of full surrender.

We can find other instances where Jesus indicated that the call to discipleship was no easy invitation. Remember when He challenged the rich young ruler to give up all his possessions and follow Jesus (Mark 10)? Or when Jesus healed someone and specifically challenged them to "go and sin no more" (John 8)? The implication was, "Because of what I've done for you, now go and live for Me. Organize your life around holiness and sacrifice for the sake of staying close to Me." We don't hear that call often enough in our churches today. Which brings us to the next factor in the rise of a cheap-grace mentality.

No One Challenges Them in Holiness

Many professing Christians never move beyond that mere profession of faith because they're not challenged to live holy lives. So many churches have allowed their sermons to morph into felt-need messages. In a culture where we must be politically correct and tolerant for fear of being canceled, it takes courage to even mention sin these days. With the rise of the seeker-sensitive church movement, sin has nearly become a taboo subject. We don't want to offend people. We don't want to sound intolerant. We don't want to sound judgmental. We don't want people to leave church upset. We want our unbelieving visitors to feel comfortable. We want to make sure we don't do or say anything that may make them decide not to return.

The Bible says, "The Word became flesh and dwelt among us. We observed his glory, the glory as the one and only Son from the Father, full of grace and truth" (John 1:14). The church must always hold grace and truth in tension as we communicate God's Word. While I agree that the gospel provides grace and hope, there are times when the people who come to church need to deal with the cutting truth of God's Word.

Why are we so afraid of challenging people in their sin? If the church doesn't challenge them to grow in purity and holiness, the world certainly won't challenge them. I'm not suggesting that every message should be fire and brimstone, but I am saying that preachers should be emboldened to preach the whole counsel of God.

CAN A PERSON GET SAVED AND NOT GROW?

This is where things get practical. Many Christians wrestle with the following questions when they encounter tension between the Bible's call to holiness and the emphasis on grace alone:

- How will I know if I'm taking advantage of God's grace?
- What if a Christian simply keeps sinning as much as they want to? Will they still go to heaven?
- Is it possible for a person to get saved and show very little fruit for the remainder of their life and still go to heaven?

To answer these questions, we must first understand how the apostle Paul classified people. In his letters he presented four categories of human beings. These are not fixed categories; there is an expected progression from one phase or category to the next. I'll explain how that progression can occur as we go, but these are the four categories: the unspiritual, the baby Christian, the carnal Christian, and the spiritual.

The Unspiritual

> The person without the Spirit does not receive what comes from God's Spirit, because it is foolishness to him; he is not able to understand it since it is evaluated spiritually.
>
> —1 CORINTHIANS 2:14

We don't need to spend much time on this group, but essentially people who are not saved through faith in Christ, through the regenerating work of the Spirit, do not have the indwelling Holy Spirit and therefore are living in sin. They don't understand spiritual things. Trying to explain things of the Spirit to them is a futile exercise because they are unable to comprehend them. The unspiritual don't need to be discipled—they need to be evangelized. When an unspiritual person is evangelized and responds in faith to the gospel, they move to the next category.

The Baby Christian

> For my part, brothers and sisters, I was not able to speak to you as spiritual people but as people of the flesh, as babies in Christ.
>
> —1 CORINTHIANS 3:1

When a person places their faith in Christ, they immediately progress from being unspiritual to being a "baby in Christ." Baby Christians have a surface-level understanding of God. But at this point in their walk that's to be expected because they are young in the faith. Just as we wouldn't expect an actual baby to understand how to add and subtract, we wouldn't expect a new Christian to understand and live out their newfound faith to the same degree a seasoned Christian would. Since they are new followers of Christ, baby Christians may struggle with sin to a much greater degree than those who are a little further down the line.

The Carnal Christian

> I gave you milk to drink, not solid food, since you were not yet ready for it. In fact, you are still not ready, because you are still worldly. For since there is envy and strife among you, are you not worldly and behaving like mere humans?
>
> —1 CORINTHIANS 3:2–3

The group we need to be especially concerned about in this discussion are carnal, or fleshly, Christians. Keep in mind that this category isn't a necessary stage of a Christian's development. Some Christians never have a season of carnality. The writer of Hebrews gives us insight into carnal Christians:

> Although by this time you ought to be teachers, you need someone to teach you the basic principles of God's revelation again. You need milk, not solid food. Now everyone who lives on milk is inexperienced with the message about righteousness, because he is an infant. But solid food is for the mature—for those whose senses have been trained to distinguish between good and evil.
>
> —HEBREWS 5:12–14

Notice several key features of the carnal Christian. According to 1 Corinthians 3, they are "worldly" and act like "mere humans" (verse 3). If you were to follow them around and observe their day-to-day actions, you would see little, if any, difference between how these Christians and unbelievers live their lives.

Hebrews 5 further diagnoses the problem: they are stuck in the baby-Christian phase. Even though they've been believers long enough that they *should* be teaching and discipling others, their growth has been stunted for one reason or another. They don't understand even the most basic Christian doctrines, which they should have mastered by now.

Is there grace for these Christians? I believe so. Paul referred to them as Christians.

Was Paul giving them license to sin? Not at all.

Was the expectation for them to remain carnal indefinitely? No.

> The baby Christians *should* be teaching and discipling others, but their growth has been stunted.

This is where we must be careful. Many have concluded that because Paul included a category for carnal Christians, it's possible for a Christian to remain in this state their entire lives. In other words, "Hey, I'm saved. I walked the aisle. I'm just one of those carnal Christians for life!"

Not so fast, buddy! I don't believe the Bible lets you get away with such an assertion. A conscious decision to embrace the life of a carnal Christian is probably an indication of deeper problems. The expectation is a progression from being a carnal Christian to becoming a spiritual Christian. Carnal Christianity is not a valid option but rather an unfortunate detour that some Christians fall into through a variety of circumstances.

The Spiritual

> The spiritual person, however, can evaluate everything, and yet he himself cannot be evaluated by anyone. For who has known the Lord's mind, that he may instruct him? But we have the mind of Christ.
>
> —1 CORINTHIANS 2:15–16

According to Paul, a spiritual Christian is so in tune with the Spirit of God that the Spirit enables them to evaluate everything that is happening from a spiritual perspective. They are spiritually equipped to evaluate speech, conduct, and even thoughts. They continually evaluate their own speech, actions, and thoughts as well as those of other people. When led by the Spirit, they are able to obtain God's perspective because they have what Paul referred to as "the mind of Christ."

We must allow for Christians to be on a continuum of sanctification. I can say that I have personally traveled through all four of these phases in my spiritual walk. At times, as a mature Christian, I've had seasons where I looked more like a carnal Christian, if I'm being honest. But those seasons were short-lived, as they should be in the life of a genuine Christian.

What does the life of a genuine Christian look like? In the following section I'll offer what I believe is an accurate depiction. As we explore the characteristics, ask yourself whether they are present in your own life.

WHAT DOES A GENUINE CHRISTIAN LOOK LIKE?

When a car isn't running the way it should, dashboard lights illuminate to alert us that there's a problem. Similarly, the Bible has many checkpoints we should pay attention to if we want to know what a healthy believer looks like.

In this section we'll unpack one beautiful passage of Scripture in 2 Peter 1 that shows precisely what should take place in the life of a believer subsequent to salvation. When a person experiences true salvation, something supernatural happens that should create several new realities in their life. As we discussed previously, the Spirit of God takes up residence in them and begins the process of sanctification. How and when that happens for people differs, but the point is that it *should* be happening. The following list isn't meant to be an exhaustive, legalistic code that we must adhere to daily. I'm simply providing it so you can assess whether these realities are happening in your life—and if not, so that you'll be equipped to ask yourself, *Why not?*

Spiritual Growth

First we see that at the moment of true conversion, God gives believers what we need to live godly, Spirit-filled lives: "His divine power has given us everything required for life and godliness through the knowledge of him who called us by his own glory and goodness. By these he has given us very great and precious promises, so that through them you may share in the divine nature, escaping the corruption that is in the world because of evil desire" (2 Peter 1:3–4). All Christians receive the same endowment—the same power and the same promises. With these we have what we need to escape the corruption in the world and grow spiritually.

Next, Peter introduces our responsibility as recipients of these gifts: "For this very reason, make every effort to supplement your faith with goodness, goodness with knowledge, knowledge with self-control, self-control with endurance, endurance with godliness, godliness with brotherly affection, and brotherly affection with love" (2 Peter 1:5–7).

God has done His part; now we must do ours. We must make *every* effort to build on our faith, goodness, knowledge, self-control, endurance, godliness, brotherly affection, and love. Notice what Peter said next: "For if you possess these qualities in increasing measure, they will keep you from being useless or unfruitful in the knowledge of our Lord Jesus Christ" (2 Peter 1:8).

There should be a clear trajectory for Christians—we should be *increasing* in each of these qualities. Many who profess to be Christians aren't growing in these areas and have remained stagnant for years upon years. Peter had something to say about such a person:

> The person who lacks these things is blind and shortsighted and has forgotten the cleansing from his past sins. Therefore, brothers and sisters, make every effort to confirm your calling and election, because if you do these things you will never stumble. For in this way, entry into the eternal kingdom of our Lord and Savior Jesus Christ will be richly provided for you.
>
> —2 Peter 1:9–11

Wow. My friend, may you and I not be lacking in these qualities. May we not be shortsighted. Peter was not suggesting that we must do these things to *get* saved or *stay* saved. That is not the point of the passage. He's saying that these things should be natural by-products of our salvation and, as such, proof that our calling and election are genuine. James made the same claim in a different way: "For just as the body without the spirit is dead, so also faith without works is dead" (James 2:26).

Spiritual Disciplines

Another sign of an authentic Christian is the presence of spiritual disciplines. I'm not suggesting that if you miss a day of Bible study, you're not saved. People can take spiritual practices too far. However, if you claim to be saved and you've *never* had a desire to engage in any spiritual disciplines, you may not be saved. The Spirit of God creates a hunger and thirst in believers to draw near to God.

By spiritual disciplines I mean activities that aid a believer in growing closer to God. Do you regularly read your Bible? Fast and pray? Worship God? Peter says that we should crave the Word of God like babies crave milk. "Like newborn infants, desire the pure milk of the word, so that by it you may grow up into your salvation" (1 Peter 2:2).

Fellowship

The Bible says that believers should be "not neglecting to gather together, as some are in the habit of doing, but encouraging each other, and all the more as you see the day approaching" (Hebrews 10:25).

> The Spirit of God creates a hunger and thirst in believers to draw near to God.

The easiest way for most Christians to gather together is getting involved in a local church. Some who profess to be Christians will also say they have no interest in church. Their excuses are typically that they had a bad experience or that church people are judgmental and hypocritical. This may be true, and yet neither of these are valid excuses for an authentic believer not to seek involvement in a church.

Let me illustrate it this way. The Bible describes the church as the bride of Christ (2 Corinthians 11:2; Ephesians 5:25–27; Revelation 19:7–9). When we reject the church, we are actually rejecting the bride of Christ. We're essentially saying, "Jesus, I love You, but I don't want to have anything to do with Your wife." We may go through seasons where we are out of fellowship, but not attending or having no desire to attend for an extended period of time is a sign of spiritual sickness for a Christian.

I can hear people saying, "Brother Allen, I don't need to go to church to be a Christian." That's true. But most people who say that also have no authentic Christian fellowship in their lives. I'll just leave you with this question: If you're not getting Christian fellowship from church, where and when is it happening?

Service

The Bible says that God has given each of us a spiritual gift: "A manifestation of the Spirit is given to each person for the common good" (1 Corinthians 12:7). Do you desire to know what your spiritual gift is, let alone use it to glorify God in His kingdom? Is there a time when you actively used your gifts in the context of a local church?

Turning from Worldly Things

As believers, we should be turning from sin and separating ourselves from worldly influences.

> Therefore, I say this and testify in the Lord: You should no longer walk as the Gentiles do, in the futility of their thoughts. They are darkened in their understanding, excluded from the life of God, because of the ignorance that is in them and because of the hardness of their hearts. They became callous and gave themselves over to promiscuity for the practice of every kind of impurity with a desire for more and more. But that is not how you came to know Christ, assuming you heard about him and were taught by him, as the truth is in Jesus, to take off your former way of life, the old self that is corrupted by deceitful desires, to be renewed in the spirit of your minds, and to put on the new self, the one created according to God's likeness in righteousness and purity of the truth.
>
> —Ephesians 4:17–24

Notice the transformation expected of Christians. Paul observed that there should be changed conduct ("walk"), changed understanding, changed behavior (abandoning promiscuity and impurity), changed desires, and a changed mindset. Other scriptures regarding our changed relationship with the world abound:

> Brothers and sisters, in view of the mercies of God, I urge you to present your bodies as a living sacrifice, holy and pleasing to God; this is your true worship. Do not be conformed to this age, but be transformed by the renewing of your mind, so that you may discern what is the good, pleasing, and perfect will of God.
>
> —ROMANS 12:1–2

> You adulterous people! Don't you know that friendship with the world is hostility toward God? So whoever wants to be the friend of the world becomes the enemy of God.
>
> —JAMES 4:4

I hope you're seeing a theme in this chapter. Salvation is free, but discipleship is costly. God desires our full surrender.

Conviction, Confession, and Repentance

Another sign of spiritual health for a genuine Christian is conviction of sin followed by confession and ultimately repentance. As Christians we will struggle with sin, but we should never surrender to it. The question is not whether we sin at all (we will) but whether we are *convicted* or *content*. Genuine Christians won't be comfortable living in sin. We will still sin, but God won't let us enjoy our sin anymore. If you are living in sin with no remorse, conviction, or desire to repent, that's a dangerous place for a professed Christian to be. Due to the dangerous nature of these false beliefs, I'm going to take my time and explain why this is critical for the believer. When it comes to conviction, confession, and repentance, people tend to gravitate toward one of two extremes.

Extreme #1: Becoming Obsessed with Asking God for Forgiveness When We Sin

You may be thinking, *Brother Allen, we do need to ask God for forgiveness. What exactly are you saying here?* You're right, but hear me out. Some people teach that our salvation is dependent on us asking for God's forgiveness. They believe that Christians exist on this slippery slope, and if we were to die immediately after committing some sin—before we have a chance to ask for forgiveness—we'd go straight to hell because we didn't repent.

A few years ago I released a video on my YouTube channel titled, "Is Suicide the Unforgivable Sin?" So many people said, "Yes, because it's the one sin you won't have time to repent from." Their assumption was that if you commit any other sin, you'll have time to ask God to forgive you. But if you commit suicide, you go to your death instantly without time to repent.

When I saw these responses, it broke my heart. It showed me that people have an incorrect view of their salvation and the nature of confession, repentance, and forgiveness. They believe the lie that their salvation is connected to their ability to remember, recount, and recite every sin they commit. They are missing the purpose of confession. We don't confess our sins to God so we can hold on to (or regain) our salvation. We confess them to receive His cleansing and restore our fellowship with Him.

Jesus gave us a beautiful picture of this in John 13:8–10. In this powerful scene He was demonstrating servant leadership for His apostles by washing their feet. As He attempted to wash Peter's feet, Peter rebuked Him: "You will never wash my feet."

"If I don't wash you, you have no part with me," Jesus replied.

At this, Peter said, "Lord, not only my feet, but also my hands and my head."

Notice Jesus' response: "One who has bathed doesn't need to wash anything except his feet, but he is completely clean. You are clean."

In those days people wore open-toed sandals, so it was common for their feet to get dirty as they traveled from place to place. But just because their feet were dirty didn't mean they needed to bathe their entire bodies. Why? Because generally speaking they were clean. It was just one body part that needed cleansing.

An understanding of Greek can help us here. In this text Jesus used two words to describe His actions. The Greek word for "wash" is *nipto*. This refers to a spot-cleaning, just as you would spot-clean a stain on a shirt.[5] The verb tense Jesus used indicates an ongoing action. People would continually need their feet to be cleansed as they walked from place to place. However, when Jesus used the word *bathed*, He switched to a different verb and tense. He used the verb *louo*, which refers to a deep cleansing of one's entire body. He also used the perfect tense, which describes "a completed verbal action that occurred in the past but which produced a state of being or a result that exists in the present (in relation to the writer). The emphasis of the perfect is not the past action so much as it is . . . the present 'state of affairs' resulting from the past action."[6]

Without going too far into the weeds in this discussion, I want to highlight that Jesus was essentially saying, "I don't need to wash your entire body. Your body is already clean. You are saved already. However, your feet are dirty and need to be washed. And they will continually need to be washed." This is such a vivid picture of our salvation. We'll get dirty along the way, but we don't need to get bathed or "resaved" when we do. We simply address the dirt we're aware of.

But the question remains, "What is the purpose of confession?" We confess our sin to God and ask His forgiveness for the same reason we do it in our other relationships. If I were to sin against my wife and never ask her to forgive me, would we still be married? Yes, of course we would be. Why? Because we entered into a covenant relationship with each other that will not be broken. But what will the *nature of our fellowship* be like when sin has occurred? It won't be healthy. It will be stained by sin. When we confess and forgive each other, our intimate fellowship is restored.

Another illustration involves clothing. For some reason, the last few times I went out to dinner with my family, I spilled food on my pants. It's actually become a running joke. Even my five-year-old daughter says, "Daddy, you stained your pants again!" When I do, I simply excuse myself from the table, go to the restroom, and put some hot water on the stain to remove it. But what I *don't* do is overreact by going home early and sending these otherwise clean pants to the cleaners. Why? Because they are already clean. I just don't want that stain there, and if I don't spot-clean it, it's a constant reminder that something is wrong and needs to be addressed.

This is the purpose of confession: We don't confess to hold on to our salvation. We confess because we've already been saved, and our hearts desire to have untainted intimacy with God.

Extreme #2: Neglecting to Ask God for Forgiveness When We Sin

The other extreme is the idea that we don't need to ask God for forgiveness at all when we sin. This reaction is built on the reasoning that if God has already forgiven our sins, what's the point of confession? Some teachers in the modern hypergrace movement promote this incorrect view, which stems from an inaccurate understanding of the value and role of confession. Let's lay down some biblical principles.

First, when we place our faith in Jesus Christ, we experience complete and total forgiveness of sins. That means we are forgiven for our past, present, and future sins. God doesn't portion out our forgiveness one confession at a time. To suggest that would be to suggest that we have to do a work (the work of confession) to maintain or contribute to our salvation. That is unscriptural.

But we need to introduce some theological terms into this conversation: *positional righteousness* and *practical righteousness*. Positional righteousness refers to how God sees us based on the work of Jesus. He sees us as righteous because we are in Christ. But we don't always live up to that calling practically speaking. In our day-to-day lives, we may or may not exemplify righteous behavior in keeping with our position in Christ. What does this mean for our current discussion? In a positional sense, there is no such thing as a believer having unforgiven sin. But from a practical standpoint, we sin against God, and that sin hinders our fellowship with Him.

Given those realities, to suggest we don't need to confess our sins to God would be as ludicrous as saying husbands and wives don't need to ask each other for forgiveness, as I stated earlier. Fellowship and intimacy are tainted when sin is introduced into the relationship.

What we need to be careful of with regard to confession is making sure we maintain the distinction between *conviction* and *condemnation*. Conviction is when the Spirit of God reminds us that we have offended God in word, thought, or deed. That is healthy. But condemnation is a feeling that originates in our hearts and pushes us further from God. It's an inner voice that says, "God doesn't want to have anything to do with you now that you've sinned. Go and feel sorry for yourself. Don't worship. Don't share your faith. Don't read your

Bible. Don't serve in church. You are banished from the presence of God for what you've done."

I'll admit that I have spent many a day in the past living in condemnation. This is not from God. But conviction is when the Spirit gently reminds you of your sin and then invites you to come to God for repentance and cleansing. The experience of conviction is laid out for us beautifully in 2 Corinthians 7:8–11.

Let's break it down verse by verse, beginning with verse 8: "Even if I grieved you with my letter, I don't regret it. And if I regretted it—since I saw that the letter grieved you, yet only for a while." Paul had written the church a letter that was apparently very stern and even somewhat harsh. Paul's rebuke grieved the people. So step one in the process of conviction is awareness. We must be made aware of our sin.

In verse 9 Paul wrote, "I now rejoice, not because you were grieved, but because your grief led to repentance. For you were grieved as God willed, so that you didn't experience any loss from us." Awareness of sin as Paul presented it created grief that led the believers to repent.

Next Paul described the difference between godly grief and worldly grief: "Godly grief produces a repentance that leads to salvation without regret, but worldly grief produces death" (verse 10). Here Paul clearly taught that godly grief or sorrow, as opposed to worldly sorrow, leads us to repentance. Why? Because we don't want our actions to hurt the heart of God.

Notice what this conviction created within the believers: "Consider how much diligence this very thing—this grieving as God wills—has produced in you: what a desire to clear yourselves, what indignation, what fear, what deep longing, what zeal, what justice! In every way you showed yourselves to be pure in this matter" (2 Corinthians 7:11). Conviction created diligence, a desire to clear themselves, indignation, fear, longing, zeal, and justice.

A critical look at the central verse on confession will help us properly understand the place it has in the life of a believer: "If we confess our sins, he is faithful and righteous to forgive us our sins and to cleanse us from all unrighteousness" (1 John 1:9). Many modern-grace preachers suggest that this verse was written not to believers but to nonbelievers. However, there is no exegetical evidence to support that conclusion. Most reputable Bible scholars agree that John's entire letter was written to believers. The promise given here is that if we confess our *known* sins to God, He is faithful to forgive them and cleanse us from *all* unrighteousness.

Dr. Tony Evans has a great illustration that explains this point. Let's say you stain your shirt. You would address that stain by spraying some stain remover on it and putting the shirt in the washing machine. But that washing machine doesn't *just* remove the stain you applied the stain remover to. It also removes all of the dirt, sweat, and other stains you didn't even know about. The result is a clean shirt. That's kind of how it works with confession. We confess the sins we know about, and God forgives these sins as well as the ones we didn't know about. So we don't need to go around all day every day confessing every little sin. We confess our sins to God as the Holy Spirit reminds us of them. It's like when you cut in front of someone in traffic and then wave your hand to the car behind you. It's not necessary, but it's customary to acknowledge the grace that has been given. This is confession.

A HEALTHY BALANCE

How do we balance everything we discussed in this chapter? We can conclude that faith alone is the means of salvation. The Bible is clear about this. The Bible is also clear about what Jesus desires in anyone who calls themselves a follower of Christ. He expects surrender, service, sacrifice, selflessness, and maybe even suffering. The Bible is replete with scriptures about what a genuine growing Christian looks like. We can also conclude that while believers may experience seasons of carnality and unfruitfulness, our lives as a whole should not be characterized this way. Conviction of sin is a healthy by-product of being in fellowship with the Spirit, which leads us to confession and ultimately repentance.

I challenge every church and every church leader to assess whether we are raising or lowering the bar when it comes to following Jesus. Are we merely inviting people to profess faith in Jesus without also challenging them to be disciples? Do we have the necessary programs in place to help them grow spiritually?

Speaking of this, the Bible also makes it clear that genuine Christians are on a continuum of becoming mature followers of Christ, and we should embrace this. There are baby Christians and carnal Christians, and there are even times when spiritual Christians will appear carnal. Genuine Christians never need to question whether they will lose their salvation, but professing Christians should examine whether they were really saved to begin with. The Bible says, "Test yourselves to see if you are in the faith. Examine yourselves. Or do you yourselves not recognize that Jesus Christ is in you?—unless you fail the test" (2 Corinthians 13:5).

I pray that those who are reading these words have received the gift of costly grace that Jesus paid the ultimate price to give us.

CONCLUSION

AN INVITATION TO DISCERNMENT

Do you want to know what happened to Jarren? Thankfully he ended up finding a solid, Bible-teaching church. He went on to become a minister and used all his negative experiences to plant a new church, where he is now faithfully teaching his congregation the Word of God every Sunday.

The moral of Jarren's story is that even though many unhealthy churches are teaching false doctrine and misleading countless numbers of people, there are also plenty of healthy, Bible-based churches out there. I am a living witness of that because I experienced many of the same things Jarren did and eventually came through to the other side. Today I'm part of a thriving, faithful church where I experience genuine fellowship with other believers, life-giving Bible teaching, and constant encouragement to draw closer to God. I am convinced that every Christian who is diligent in their search will discover the right church in time. Notice I didn't say *perfect*! No church is perfect, but it will be right for you.

Many false teachings are circulating around the body of Christ today. Solid Bible teachers won't be able to track them all down, no matter how hard we try. Above and beyond anything else I could pray for you as we conclude our journey together is that this book has taught you the importance of having discernment. Not everyone who says, "I believe in Jesus" is a Christian. Not everyone who uses Bible verses to support what they believe is teaching truth. We all need to be more like the believers of the Berean church of whom it was said, "The people here were of more noble character than those in Thessalonica, since they received the word with eagerness and examined the Scriptures daily to see if these things were so" (Acts 17:11).

Like the Bereans, don't take everything I've written in this book at face value! Ask God to give you a discerning heart as you compare my words against the inerrant, trustworthy words of the Bible.

I trust God will lead you to the truth.

RECOMMENDED RESOURCES

There are so many excellent resources available that can inform and encourage you on your journey toward discernment—these are just a few to help get you started. Even so, sometimes I hesitate to make recommendations because, outside of the Bible, every author and every book has flaws and blind spots. So while I believe these contain lots of good guidance and insights, let me just add this disclaimer: a *recommendation* isn't an *endorsement* of every claim or teaching in these books! While I hope you find these resources beneficial, I urge you to test everything against Scripture, with the help of prayer and godly counsel. I believe that as you engage in prayerful study, your discernment—and faith—will grow.

PROPHECY, SPEAKING IN TONGUES, AND OTHER SPIRITUAL GIFTS

Are Miraculous Gifts for Today? 4 Views in The Counterpoints series, edited by Stanley N. Gundry (Zondervan, 1996).

Wayne Grudem, *The Gift of Prophecy in the New Testament and Today* (Crossway, 2000).

Sam Storms, *Understanding Spiritual Gifts: A Comprehensive Guide* (Zondervan, 2020).

HEALTH, WEALTH, AND MANIFESTATION

Costi W. Hinn, *God, Greed, and the (Prosperity) Gospel* (Zondervan, 2019).

Tara Sun, *Surrender Your Story: Ditch the Myth of Control and Discover Freedom in Trusting God* (Thomas Nelson, 2023).

Holly Pivec and R. Douglas Geivett, *Counterfeit Kingdom: The Dangers of New Revelation, New Prophets, and New Age Practices in the Church* (Broadman & Holman, 2022).

GRACE, LEGALISM, AND SALVATION

Four Views on Salvation in a Pluralistic World in The Counterpoints series, edited by Stanley N. Gundry (Zondervan, 1996).

Four Views on Eternal Security in The Counterpoints series, edited by Stanley N. Gundry (Zondervan, 2002).

Ruth Chou Simons, *When Strivings Cease: Replacing the Gospel of Self-Improvement with the Gospel of Life-Transforming Grace* (Thomas Nelson, 2021).

SPIRITUAL ABUSE

Michael J. Kruger, *Confronting the Problem of Spiritual Abuse in the Church* (Zondervan, 2022).

David Johnson and Jeff VanVonderen, *The Subtle Power of Spiritual Abuse: Recognizing and Escaping Spiritual Manipulation and False Spiritual Authority Within the Church* (Bethany House, 2005).

PROGRESSIVE CHRISTIANITY

Alisa Childers, *Another Gospel? A Lifelong Christian Seeks Truth in Response to Progressive Christianity* (Tyndale, 2020).

ACKNOWLEDGMENTS

There are many people that I could acknowledge in this book. I want to especially acknowledge my dear mother, who sacrificed so much as a single mom working several jobs to provide my sister and me with a wonderful quality of life. She has been a constant source of support for me. I would also like to acknowledge my father, who gave me my first Bible and led me to the Lord at the tender age of eight. As a minister himself, he set the example for me to follow. I will forever be grateful for his deposit of ministry into my life.

But the person I need to acknowledge and thank the most is my dear and loving wife. I've always wanted to be a present father and a loving husband, but over this past year I needed to spend countless weekends at hotels simply writing for hours while she cared for our two little children. She sacrificed so much to give me time away from home to write this book. Jennifer, I will forever be grateful for your sacrifice and commitment to me and our children. You are the real hero and superstar of our family.

NOTES

Chapter 1: I Haven't Spoken in Tongues. Am I Missing Out?

1. Walter Bauer, *A Greek-English Lexicon of the New Testament and Other Early Christian Literature*, 3rd ed., ed. Frederick William Danker (Chicago: University of Chicago Press, 2000), s.v. "glossa."
2. Bauer, *Greek-English Lexicon*, s.v. "dialekto."
3. "What the Bible Says About Charis," Forerunner Commentary, Bible Tools, accessed February 7, 2023, https://www.bibletools.org/index.cfm/fuseaction/topical.show/rtd/cgg/id/518/charis.htm.
4. For example, see David Jeremiah, *God in You: Releasing the Power of the Holy Spirit in Your Life* (New York: Crown Publishing Group, 2013), 96.

Chapter 2: Are Health and Wealth Guaranteed for All the Faithful?

1. Robert Tilton, *God's Word About Prosperity* (Dallas: Word of Faith Publications, 1983), 6.
2. "What Did Jesus Mean When He Told People, 'Your Faith Has Made You Well'?," Got Questions, accessed January 24, 2023, https://www.gotquestions.org/your-faith-has-made-you-well.html.
3. Max Roser, "The Short History of Global Living Conditions and Why It Matters That We Know," Our World in Data, last updated 2020, https://ourworldindata.org/a-history-of-global-living-conditions-in-5-charts.
4. Paula White, *Living the Abundant Life: Why Not Me? Why Not Now?* (Tampa, FL: Paula White Ministries, 2003), 24, https://books.google.com/books?newbks=1&newbks_redir=0&id=t7co-mKHaE8C&dq.

5. Kenneth Copeland, *The Laws of Prosperity* (Fort Worth, TX: Kenneth Copeland Publications, 1974), 19.

6. David W. Jones and Russell S. Woodbridge, *Health, Wealth & Happiness: Has the Prosperity Gospel Overshadowed the Gospel of Christ?* (Grand Rapids, MI: Kregel, 2011), 89.

7. Kenneth Copeland, *The Troublemaker* (Fort Worth, TX: Kenneth Copeland Publications, 1996), 6.

8. Stephen R. Covey (@stephenrcovey), "You can't talk your way out of a problem," Twitter, August 8, 2017, 8:45 a.m., https://twitter.com /stephenrcovey/status/894932530561986560.

9. Gloria Copeland, *God's Will Is Prosperity* (Tulsa, OK: Harrison House, 1982), 54. Mark 10:29–30 records Jesus' comment that those who leave behind their homes, families, and possessions "for me and for the gospel will . . . receive a hundred times as much in this present age." But as is always the case with interpreting the Bible, individual verses must be understood in context and in light of the overall message of Scripture.

10. Shayne Lee, *T. D. Jakes: America's New Preacher* (New York: New York University Press, 2005), 110–11.

11. Laurie Goodstein, "Believers Invest in the Gospel of Getting Rich," *New York Times*, August 16, 2009, A1, https://www.nytimes.com/2009/08/16 /us/16gospel.html.

12. David Pilgrim, "Egoism or Altruism: A Social Psychological Critique of the Prosperity Gospel of Televangelist Robert Tilton," *Journal of Religious Studies* 18, no. 1/2 (1990): 3, quoted in David Jones, "The Bankruptcy of the Prosperity Gospel: An Exercise in Biblical and Theological Ethics," Bible.org, October 6, 2006, https://bible.org/article /bankruptcy-prosperity-gospel-exercise-biblical-and-theological-ethics #P10_2696.

13. Jones and Woodbridge, *Health, Wealth & Happiness*, 107.

14. Joyce Meyer, *Healing Scriptures* (Fenton, MO: Joyce Meyer Ministries, 2008), 5, 8, available at Faith and Health Connection, PDF, accessed January 30, 2023, https://www.faithandhealthconnection.org/wp -content/uploads/Healing-Scriptures-Joyce-Meyers.pdf.

Chapter 3: Do I Really Have the Power to Speak Things into Existence?

1. "Is There Power in Positive Confession?," Got Questions, accessed January 25, 2023, https://www.gotquestions.org/positive-confession .html.

2. David W. Jones and Russell S. Woodbridge, *Health, Wealth & Happiness: Has the Prosperity Gospel Overshadowed the Gospel of Christ?* (Grand Rapids, MI: Kregel, 2011), 26.

3. Phineas Parkhurst Quimby, *The Quimby Manuscripts*, 2nd ed., ed. Horatio W. Dresser (New York: Thomas Y. Crowell, 1921), 186.

4. Ralph Waldo Trine, *In Tune with the Infinite* (New York: Thomas Y. Crowell, 1897), 176–77.

5. Trine, *In Tune with the Infinite*, 42.

6. Jones and Woodbridge, *Health, Wealth & Happiness*, 43.

7. Trine, *In Tune with the Infinite*, 84.

8. Creflo Dollar, "The Creative Power of Words," sermon, Creflo Dollar Ministries, College Park, GA, June 30, 2021, YouTube video, 36:55, https://www.youtube.com/watch?v=Hves55PxcJs.

9. Earl Paulk, *Satan Unmasked* (Atlanta: K Dimension, 1984), 96–97, https://books.google.com/books?id=4QLjZTMpYEMC.

10. Kenneth Copeland, "The Force of Love" (Fort Worth, TX: Kenneth Copeland Ministries, 1987, audiotape #02–0028), side 1, quoted in Hank Hanegraaff and Erwin M. de Castro, "What's Wrong with the Faith Movement? (Part Two): The Teachings of Kenneth Copeland," *Christian Research Journal* 15, no. 4 (1993), http://www.equip.org/PDF /JAW755-2.pdf.

11. Joyce Meyer, "Little Gods," published by Kerrigan Skelly, July 12, 2007, audio file, YouTube, 4:47, https://www.youtube.com /watch?v=7Y4eVu2oxP8.

12. Kenneth Hagin, *Word of Faith* (December 1980), 14, https://events .rhema.org/wof/.

13. Donald M. Williams, *Psalms 73–150*, vol. 14 of The Preacher's Commentary, ed. Lloyd J. Ogilvie (Nashville: Thomas Nelson, 1989), 90.

14. "Is There Power in Positive Confession?," Got Questions.

15. "Is 'Name It Claim It' Teaching Biblical?," Got Questions, accessed January 25, 2023, https://www.gotquestions.org/name-it-claim-it.html.

16. Vivian Bricker, "Is Manifesting Our Lives for the Better Biblical?,"
Christianity.com, June 28, 2021, https://www.christianity.com/wiki
/christian-life/is-manifesting-our-lives-for-the-better-biblical.html.

Chapter 4: What About Prophets and Prophecy?

1. John Piper, "When Will Prophecy Cease?," Desiring God, March 18,
1990, https://www.desiringgod.org/messages/when-will-prophecy
-cease.
2. Piper, "When Will Prophecy Cease?"
3. "Is the Gift of Prophecy Still Available for the Church?," Blue Letter
Bible, accessed January 26, 2023, https://www.blueletterbible.org
/Comm/stewart_don/faq/the-various-gifts-of-the-holy-spirit/12
-is-the-gift-of-prophecy-still-available-for-the-church.cfm.
4. John Piper, "The Authority and Nature of the Gift of Prophecy,"
Desiring God, March 25, 1990, https://www.desiringgod.org/messages
/the-authority-and-nature-of-the-gift-of-prophecy.
5. Piper, "Authority and Nature of the Gift of Prophecy."
6. "Were the New Testament Prophetic Messages Given Without Error?,"
Blue Letter Bible, accessed January 26, 2023, https://www
.blueletterbible.org/Comm/stewart_don/faq/the-various-gifts
-of-the-holy-spirit/10-were-the-new-testament-prophetic-messages
-given-without-error.cfm.
7. John F. Walvoord and Roy B. Zuck, eds., *The Bible Knowledge
Commentary: New Testament* (Colorado Springs: David C. Cook, 1983),
733.
8. Piper, "Authority and Nature of the Gift of Prophecy."

Chapter 5: What Does Progressive Christianity Teach?

1. LeRon Shults, quoted in Tony Jones, *The New Christians: Dispatches
from the Emergent Frontier* (Minneapolis: Fortress Press, 2019),
234–35.
2. Alisa Childers, *Another Gospel? A Lifelong Christian Seeks Truth
in Response to Progressive Christianity* (Carol Stream, IL: Tyndale
Momentum, 2020), 74.
3. For a helpful overview, see Alisa Childers, "How We Got Here: A
History of Progressive Christianity," Impact 360 Institute, accessed

January 26, 2023, https://www.impact360institute.org/articles/progressive-christianity-history/.

4. "What Is Deconstruction? What Does It Mean When People Say They Are Deconstructing Their Faith?," Got Questions, accessed January 26, 2023, https://www.gotquestions.org/deconstruction.html.

5. Michael Kruger, "What Is Progressive Christianity?," Reformed Theological Seminary, November 3, 2020, https://rts.edu/resources/what-is-progressive-christianity/.

6. "What Is Progressive Christianity?," Bethel Congregational United Church of Christ, accessed January 26, 2023, https://www.bethelbeaverton.org/progressive-christianity.

7. "About Us," Church of the Foothills, https://www.churchofthefoothills.org/about-us/progressive-christianity/. Church of the Foothills' statement regarding Jesus is no longer posted on the website as of January 26, 2023.

8. Carl Krieg, "Who Was Jesus? Part Two," ProgressiveChristianity.org, June 26, 2019, https://progressivechristianity.org/resources/who-was-jesus-part-two/.

9. "The Core Values of Progressive Christianity," ProgressiveChristianity.org, updated 2022, https://progressivechristianity.org/the-8-points.

10. "What Is Progressive Christianity?," Bethel, emphasis added.

11. "What Is Progressive Christianity?," Bethel.

12. "What Is Progressive Christianity?," Bethel.

13. Alisa Childers, "What Do Progressive Christians Believe?," White Horse Inn, February 10, 2021, https://whitehorseinn.org/resource-library/articles/what-do-progressive-christians-believe/.

14. "Our Story," BELOVED Way, accessed February 21, 2023, https://belovedway.org/who-we-are/our-story/.

15. "Progressive Christianity," Parkview United Church of Christ, accessed February 7, 2023, https://www.mnparkviewucc.org/progressive-christianity.html.

16. "Open and Affirming," Wikipedia, last modified December 30, 2022, https://en.wikipedia.org/wiki/Open_and_affirming.

17. "We Welcome the LGBTQ Community to Participate in the Full Life of Our Church," Bethel Congregational United Church of Christ, accessed January 26, 2023, https://www.bethelbeaverton.org/what-does-the-bible-say-about-homosexuality.

18. James Burklo, "Choice Sanctuary," ProgressiveChristianity.org, May 5, 2022, https://progressivechristianity.org/resources/choice-sanctuary/.

19. "Chapter 2. The Second Commandment: Gross Sin Forbidden," in The Didache, trans. M. B. Riddle, in vol. 7 of Ante-Nicene Fathers, ed. Alexander Roberts, James Donaldson, and A. Cleveland Coxe (Buffalo, NY: Christian Literature Publishing Co., 1886), archived at New Advent, https://www.newadvent.org/fathers/0714.htm.

20. "About Us," Church of the Foothills.

21. "What Is Progressive Christianity?," Bethel.

22. "What Is Progressive Christianity?," Bethel.

23. "Strong's Greek: 2315. Theopneustos," Bible Hub, accessed February 2, 2023, https://biblehub.com/greek/2315.htm.

24. Warren W. Wiersbe, Be Ready: Living in Light of Christ's Return, 2nd. ed. (Colorado Springs: David C. Cook, 2010), 71.

25. "What Does the Bible Say About Homosexuality?," Bethel Congregational United Church of Christ, accessed January 27, 2023, https://www.bethelbeaverton.org/what-does-the-bible-say-about -homosexuality.

26. "What Does the Bible Say About Homosexuality?," Bethel.

27. Kirstie Piper, "Science vs. Bible: When Does Life Begin?," Focus on the Family, June 21, 2021, https://www.focusonthefamily.com/pro-life /pre-brn/science-vs-bible-when-does-life-begin/.

28. Jeffrey Frantz, "Beyond Atonement Theology: Letting Go of the Mantra: 'Jesus Died for Our Sins,'" ProgressiveChristianity.org, May 4, 2020, https://progressivechristianity.org/resources/beyond-atonement -theology/.

29. Frantz, "Beyond Atonement Theology."

Chapter 6: Can I Lose My Salvation?

1. Charles Haddon Spurgeon, "Sermon 820: Working Out What Is Worked In," in Sermons of Rev. C. H. Spurgeon, vol. 14, 1868 (New York: Funk and Wagnalls, 1883), https://www.spurgeongems.org/sermon /chs820.pdf.

2. "Strong's Greek: 3762. Oudeis and Outheis, Oudemia, Ouden, and Outhen," Bible Hub, accessed February 7, 2023, https://biblehub.com /greek/3762.htm.

3. Beau Lee, *Jesus Plus Nothing Equals Salvation* (New York: Mind Massive, 2017).

4. Horatio G. Spafford, "It Is Well with My Soul," music by Philip P. Bliss, in *Gospel Hymns No. 2* (1876), archived at Hymnary, https://hymnary.org/text/when_peace_like_a_river_attendeth_my_way.

5. "Strong's Greek: 166. Aionios," Bible Hub, accessed February 7, 2023, https://biblehub.com/greek/166.htm.

6. Walter Bauer, *A Greek-English Lexicon of the New Testament and Other Early Christian Literature*, 3rd ed., ed. Frederick William Danker (Chicago: University of Chicago Press, 2000), 117.

7. Bauer, *Greek-English Lexicon*, 155.

Chapter 7: Can I Be Saved and Not Be a Disciple?

1. Dietrich Bonhoeffer, *The Cost of Discipleship* (New York: Touchstone, 1995), 43.

2. Bonhoeffer, *Cost of Discipleship*, 43–45.

3. Robbie F. Castleman, "The Skim-Milk Gospel of Cheap Grace," *Themelios* 30, no. 1 (September 2004), https://www.thegospelcoalition.org/themelios/article/the-skim-milk-gospel-of-cheap-grace/.

4. American Bible Society, *State of the Bible 2021*, cited in "State of the Bible 2021: Five Key Findings," Barna Research, May 19, 2021, https://www.barna.com/research/sotb-2021/.

5. "Strong's Greek: 3538. Nipto," Bible Hub, accessed February 7, 2023, https://biblehub.com/greek/3538.htm.

6. Michael S. Heiser and Vincent M. Setterholm, *Glossary of Morpho-Syntactic Database Terminology* (Bellingham, WA: Lexham Press, 2013), s.v. "louo."

ABOUT THE AUTHOR

Allen Parr is a national speaker, YouTuber, author, ordained minister, husband, and father. He is the cofounder (with his wife, Jennifer) of Let's Equip, a nonprofit organization that equips Christians and Christian organizations with courses and curriculum to aid in biblical literacy and spiritual growth. Allen is a proud graduate of Dallas Theological Seminary, where he earned his master of theology degree in 2004. He has served on staff at several churches in various positions, including worship pastor and pastor of Christian education. His popular YouTube channel, The BEAT (Biblical Encouragement And Truth) with Allen Parr, reaches millions of believers with encouragement to live out their true calling as Christians. He and Jennifer and their two children live in Texas.